Stories
from the
Heart

The Walk *of a* Widow

Lillian Adrian

WESTBOW
PRESS®
A DIVISION OF THOMAS NELSON
& ZONDERVAN

WestBow Press books may be ordered through booksellers or by contacting:

WestBow Press
A Division of Thomas Nelson & Zondervan
1663 Liberty Drive
Bloomington, IN 47403
www.westbowpress.com
844-714-3454

ISBN: 978-1-6642-4353-8 (sc)
ISBN: 978-1-6642-4354-5 (hc)
ISBN: 978-1-6642-4352-1 (e)

Library of Congress Control Number: 2021917703

Print information available on the last page.

WestBow Press rev. date: 01/11/2022

Pain insists upon being attended to. God whispers to us in our pleasures, speaks in our conscience, but shouts in our pain: it is His megaphone to rouse a deaf world. We are most keenly aware of God's character in our suffering. It is when our self-sufficiency is peeled away that we see how weak we really are.

—C. S. Lewis

Contents

Foreword... xi

Preface xiii

Acknowledgments xvii

Introduction...xxvii

Chapter 1   The Walk of a Widow 1
Chapter 2   My New Kind of Normal 8
Chapter 3   Reality Revealed 15
Chapter 4   God's Hand, from the Outside Looking In..................... 23
Chapter 5   Lord, Where Are You Calling Me?.................................. 30
Chapter 6   The Real Journey Begins... 31
Chapter 7   Aloneness, the Next Step 43
Chapter 8   The Process of Healing.. 48
Chapter 9   The Promises... 58
Chapter 10 From Why to What 63
Chapter 11 Faith, Not Feelings 71
Chapter 12 Today Is Tomorrow's Yesterday 81
Chapter 13 His Awesomeness Revealed... 86
Chapter 14 What Is Your Story?... 91
Chapter 15 Living with Purpose Again 94

Foreword

Every once in a while, a book simply grabs you by the heart, and you don't want to put it down.

I felt this way about *Stories from the Heart: The Walk of a Widow*.

From the very first page, Lilly's story captured every ounce of me because I know the author well; I am her first cousin, and she is my dearest friend in all the world. I have watched her live her story out loud for more than sixty years.

I have watched her walk as a girl, woman, wife, mother, and fellow sojourner through all life's seasons and have experienced her passion and joy for living that is unsurpassed.

I have born witness to the testimony of her life.

Lilly's story has always been full of life at its best. Her story continues in this book at a point where someone else's story ends, a wonderful man named Tim. He was deeply loved by Lilly, and her grief for his loss is palpable as you read each word.

The scar on her heart will forever remain, and the imprint of Tim's legacy of love is seen in the lives of his precious daughters and grandchildren. They carry him in their hearts, and Tim's spirit lives on.

He is ever present in "heart memory," as evidenced in the many daily nuances of life that go on, long after any of us is gone.

If a picture paints a thousand words, then a thousand words on these pages will paint a picture in your own heart.

Real. Raw. Truthful. Tearful. Triumphant.

Terribly sad and wonderfully uplifting.

These words don't do proper justice to the impact of her story's affect on me. As a fellow human being on my own journey, I related to so many of the stories I read; some resonated more than others and a few, more deeply than I could have imagined.

Lilly's anecdotal style of sharing moments of abject pain in losing her precious Tim unexpectedly, and her utter and complete dependence on the Lord for guidance and comfort are found in every chapter.

Her rich love of God's Word is shared for readers to reference on their own unique journeys. I found true comfort in this aspect and will refer to this book again and again in days to come.

This heart-wrenching, life-changing, and tumultuous season of her life is documented on every page, yet even more important, so too is her deep faith in God's sustaining love, grace, and mercy, as evidenced in her acceptance of the inevitable fact that this "widow's walk" in losing Tim belongs to her and her alone.

Her stories are heartbreaking in places, and in others, gloriously redemptive to the human spirit in need of comfort when losing someone loved with all one's heart.

Lilly's journey will change your life forever, if you let it.

I pray you will find comfort between the covers of this book. Anyone who has lost a loved one can benefit from reading her beautiful collection of stories from the heart.

Prepare to be blessed and, perhaps, inspired to begin writing stories of your own.

I thank God for Lilly's continued testimony of love and for reminding my own heart to trust the Lord in all things.

—Marti Jolly Miller

Preface

I have been writing this book for fourteen years. The reason is simple: after fourteen years, I can finally get some closure on the most devastating moment in my life.

I hope that as you read this book, you will understand the importance of closure—not forgetting but getting closure to pain—and openness to completeness, hope, joy, and peace again.

For me, *nothing* was worse than losing the love of my life. So many people rallied around me for that moment, but then their words began ringing in my ears: "Don't worry. You will someday soon find that new kind of normal."

I have been searching for fourteen long years to find a "new kind of normal," and let me just say this: there isn't one. There is recognition of life gone and of new beginnings, with new memories. Well, maybe that *is* a new kind of normal.

I realize there is hope, joy, and peace in knowing, without a shadow of a doubt, that my heavenly Father loves me more than life itself. That is where I gain my trust. His Word is clear on that in John 3:16. Normal is different for everyone. And for me, there was nothing normal about losing my spouse so suddenly when he was fifty-four; then again, there is nothing normal about dying on a cross for my sins and yours. What's normal about a kind and gentle man being crucified; spit upon; beaten until blood ran down His face, hands, and sides; cursed; and then left to hang on an old rugged cross while His mother sat and watched, weeping for the loss of her son. But she too had hope, joy, and peace, knowing her heavenly Father loved her more that day than the day before. Even though she knew it was not a normal kind of death, she knew it was right in the eyes of God and that He ordained it as His will and that His perfect plan was coming into place three short days later. Glory be to God in the highest (Job 19:25).

Now, mine has not been three short days, but then again, I am certain that Jesus felt as though it was years as He experienced the torture and uttered those last words, "It is finished" (John 19:30 TLB).

And when all was said and done with Tim's life those words too were spoken: "It is finished"

But that's where we gain our hope, joy, and peace; we know, deep in our spirits, that we too will rise up into the heavens one day. That day will be here in the twinkle of an eye if the one we love knows God personally, as Tim knew Him and as our girls and I know Him. Then the grand reunion will be soon!

One thing I have to say about the walk of a widow is that there is no journey too deep or too long that Jesus cannot hold us up and get us through the valley of the shadow of death. Have you heard the word *Paraclete*? Look it up; it will bless you beyond measure. Jesus wants desperately to be that Paraclete for you.

As His Word says in John 3:16, one of the simplest yet most powerful scriptures we ever memorized as little children, "For God so loved the world that He gave His only begotten son, that whosoever believes in Him shall not perish but have everlasting life" (KJV).

I will never forget the words my daddy said to me on that horrible day when Tim died, April 21, 2007: "Lillian Anne, Tim is more alive today than he has ever been before. We will all see him again, and what a glorious day that will be."

Death used to scare me but not anymore.

We are just the shell that holds in the good stuff. One day, I will never have to worry about eating alone, worshipping alone, or having that morning cup of coffee alone. I won't have to worry about losing ten pounds or being lonely. I will be whole.

And one day, I will hold two of my grandbabies, whom I never got to meet, in my arms, knowing their Papa Tim has played with them for hours upon hours, up and down golden streets in heaven.

The pain that Casey and Damon and Kelly and Chalon (my daughters and their husbands) experienced was above what I could have imagined. They were patient with me as I grieved and stood by my side, trying hard to fix me. I am so sorry I did not take the time to understand their grief, as I know it was deep and hard. No amount of research can capture this distinctly painful and powerful grief, as it affects each of us differently. The emotional trauma can be devastating for your child, even as a young adult. They lose some of their own identity. I did not recognize this and instead felt as though I was the only one in pain, even as they ached inside. They graciously took the responsibility of assisting me through my journey, although I did not recognize their need for assurance and validation and that it was OK for them to also hurt and cry. Getting me back to a normal state of existence became their priority. Because of their undeniable strength in the Lord, they allowed me to grieve as I needed, to become somewhat healthy again, and to know that hope, joy, and peace would soon enter my heart through my trust in God. If not for that, I am not sure I would be the person I am today. Another great blessing from the Lord is my precious children.

Recognizing the pain from grief and the true depth of it helps us to grasp the hard journey before us; that journey also belongs to the others who also loved the person who died, but it's only normal that we are consumed with our own grief and sometimes overlook the grief that others are feeling.

Perhaps if we shared our grief with others who are also experiencing this great pain, our personal grief would become less painful.

We generally think of grief as a reaction to death, but grief is the process of accepting the unacceptable.

Because of the deep pain, we do all we can to avoid it and escape it through placing our energies in a different direction. Don't get me wrong; that's not all bad. We must find ways to survive, and finding other outlets for our grief makes this possible. The process of grieving normally depends on the type of loss. If it's a spouse, the pain will often seem intensified because of the guilt, anger, anxiety, loneliness, and sense of despair. Also, because we cannot fix it. Often, as it was in my case, when death is sudden, we spend much time in denial. This too shall pass and heal and get better. Then the shock of reality it is final.

Then comes the confusion and pain of needing answers, searching for *why*.

Well-meaning friends may say to you, "It will fade quickly. The pain will go away. Just give yourself a little time." You might want to meet their expectations, but you can't. It is *your* pain, and while they can empathize with you, they never can feel what you are feeling.

Much of the grieving process and the way we walk through it can depend on our support systems, our spiritual beliefs, our families, and our friends.

Throughout this book, I mention all of the above in my journey; without each piece of this puzzle, I could not have made it.

I depended greatly on my heavenly Father. Well, I worked hard at depending on him. In the beginning, I did not like Him much. After all, I had to find someone to blame, and Tim was gone, so God was next. He got the brunt of my anger and bitterness.

Now, let me share my journey and how it helped me to realize there are no longer *why* questions but only *what* questions. I ask, "What, precious Father, do you want from me at this time in my life? Let me be a vessel for you to bring people to the foot of the cross that you so lovingly sacrificed yourself for. I humble myself before you to serve you and to minister to those who walk the walk of a widow."

Lord, let me find rainbows daily to see Your promises of love and protection of me.

Had it not been for God's amazing grace, I would not be able to share with you these *Stories from the Heart.*

Acknowledgments

Blessed are those who mourn, for they will be comforted.

—Matthew 5:4 (KJV)

When you wake up one morning and all the things you never expected to happen—things that only happen to other people—are staring you in the face, your heart feels as though it is in a million pieces, never to be whole again. There is no way to walk through a tragedy such as the death of a spouse without the people who love you unconditionally stepping up and carrying you through the journey. That's the main reason I could write *Stories from the Heart.* I call these amazing friends and dear family members my *Paracletes*, as the Bible calls them—those who lift you up when you can no longer walk. Their willingness to listen to my story, repeatedly, was a *must* for me to heal. The love and understanding that they gave me so unconditionally was beyond my deepest comprehension. When all the cards and casseroles were gone, they were not. When all life's daily schedules returned to normal, and mine was far from normal, they were still there. When the stillness of the night and the long, enduring weekends shook my very being, they held me tight.

Finding the right words to share my heart is so difficult, but I thank them for loving me throughout this journey of deep grief, as I searched daily for rainbows. They became one of God's most radiant promises of His love and protection over me. It is those folks who enter our lives, for either a season or forever, who complete us and teach us how to be survivors of those tumultuous and violent disturbances in our lives, through which we could not have journeyed without their strong hands and God's abiding love for us.

First and foremost, Father God, I praise you. I worship you. I thank you for your faithfulness to never let me go and for always forgiving me for the doubt, fear, anger, and disobedience to your Word. Yet you held me close to your heart and protected me. For my eternal salvation and saving me by grace, I thank you.

To my precious daughters, Casey and Kelly and their precious husbands: how can I say thanks for your love like none other? You stood by me and walked the entire journey with me. You did all you possibly could to protect me from the pain that was inevitable. You too were dying inside, but you always put me first. Your strength, despite your grief, was what I saw. Your passion and love for my well-being was so evident in all your actions. Forgive me for not being more sensitive to your great loss.

Thank you for loving me, standing beside me, moving me from pillar to post, and being all that was needed of you during that time.

To Blakely, Ellis, Cannon, Beckett, and Briggs, my precious grandchildren: you are the sunshine of my life, and you would have been for your Papa Tim also. He always dreamed about you and prayed for you, that you would be healthy, strong, giggle a lot, and know the Lord. His dreams and prayers are unfolding in you each day. You truly complete my very being. I love you so much.

To my brother Jim: you became my everyday confidant, the one I knew would always lift me up and hold me when I could not walk. You held my shaken world and steadied it for me. You reminded me every day that I was not forgotten and that I was vital in many lives. You have always made sure that I knew you would always be there, no matter what. You were the glue that held my broken pieces in place. As I pulled those bandages off, ever so gently, a little at a time, you never left me feeling alone. I will love and respect you forever.

To my sister, Ladye: you taught me the meaning of *tears of love*—such reassurance in a time when tears were many. You gently reminded me that with every teardrop, Tim was praying for me. Sisters will always be sisters, and we have walked through many storms together and always pulled each other through. We have many stories to tell—some that we won't tell and others that warm my heart when I think of them so fondly. I love you and am so grateful that God blessed me with you.

To my brothers Harry, and John: thank you for supporting me and encouraging me as you stood by my side. Harry, for picking up my tab often, when my finances were slim, for packing and unpacking me a time or two, and to you both, for standing in the gap with me during those final moments of Tim's life, when I knew it was hard for you to stand. From that kindergarten moment, John, when only my kiss could get you through your day, a bond was born.

To my sweet parents, Fred and Maxine, who are enjoying heaven's gifts with Tim at this very moment. You wrapped your arms around me as only parents can do and assured me that Tim was more alive today than ever before. You loved my husband and supported me as I lost him. Your home became my place of rest, once those moments became so quiet. Thank you. I will love you forever, and I miss you greatly.

To Mike and Kay: you truly were your brother's best friend. Tim loved you so much. Mike, you stood by Tim's bed, day after day, never leaving my side or the girl's side. You would talk to Tim, even though Tim was asleep or comatose toward the end. You continued to reminisce with him on wonderful times together as a brother, fishing, the deer lease, California life together, and so much more. You wanted to make sure that *if* Tim could hear you that he would know the deep abiding love you had for him, as you reminded Tim of Kay's love too.

Thank you for never leaving the hospital during those three long weeks, for standing by Tim's side, and for continuing to speak words of encouragement to him and tell funny stories that only the two of you shared, as well as the love that only brothers can have for each other. I am so grateful to have you and Kay as my family. You continue every day, loving us and helping us to continue to realize why we are so blessed to be Adrians.

To Susan: Tim loved you to the Lord. He was always so grateful that he could be a part of that special moment in your life. Thank you for being there in the room with him as he took his last breath. He knew you were there and that you loved him more than life itself.

To Mimi and Dandy: you too are celebrating life with Tim in heaven today. He loved you both so much. I can only imagine the pain you must have felt, losing your son. I know the ache in your hearts was deep. Thank you for sharing him with us for over thirty years. Mimi, thank you for many chocolate chip cookies and for sharing with us the secret recipe. Those cookies have brought all of us much peace during times of great need. I miss you both so much.

To my sweet cousin Marti: I will always be so grateful for that day that you answered your phone and walked right back into my life when I needed you the most. We shared so many precious memories as children in Pittsburgh, but the memories and times we share now are above all else. Thank you for always being there for me, my cheerleader and encourager always. You are the one person I could always depend on, always bringing to my attention the persons we should be in the Lord and that we were Jollys for a reason. You taught me to wear God's Spirit and His love in a way that others would know He was real in my life when that was so difficult to do. You gave me the courage to look up instead of down and to know I was never going to stand alone. Thank you for helping me to complete this book, reading its every word in the first drafts, and affirming to me that this was certainly part of God's plan for my healing and perhaps the healing of many other hearts with similar stories. Thank you for writing the foreword of this book. I love you, Marti, my cousin, my friend.

To my stronghold and confidant, Verdell Davis, my sweet, sweet friend: when Kelly called the church and said, "My daddy died, and we need help," they directed us to you. Thank you for those moments in your sunroom as you grieved with me and wept, remembering your own journey of grief. I have shared your book, *Let Me Grieve but Not Forever* with hundreds of people, in grocery store lines, in airports, in restaurants, at soccer games, and even at a memorial service of a man I loved dearly. How could I do that? I always keep ten copies at close range. That book was what truly brought me through this nightmare. You showed me I could find joy again and still hold Tim close to my heart. Thank you.

To my enormous group of friends: thank you to those friends who touched me every day, who loved Tim and respected him. The list is so long. Some of you walked every moment, from that original call until this very day. You have held me close in your heart.

To Pete and Cathy: how will I ever be able to thank you properly for carrying me every step of the way? Pete, your visual love during those first moments in that dark room, when we heard the words from the doctor—"He is never going to be who he was, if he even survives"—you said it so well: "Only God has the last word." Then you took a step further to explain to me what that meant, once Tim was gone. "God's last word is not always the words we want to hear, but they are mighty, and He never lets us go." I know I am older than you (as you remind me each year), but you were wiser than I was to see God's hand in all that took place at the time. I love you, my friend.

Cathy, thanks for many cups of coffee, for allowing me to use the most comfortable bed in your home for months, for praying for me and for Tim during our darkest hours, for being my true best friend, and for knowing God's Word and gently explaining it to me. Honestly, Cathy, there are no words to express to you and Pete how much I love you and appreciate you for all you have come to mean in my life.

Thank you for sharing your heart and soul in this book with me. It is what completes my story.

Thanks for entering my estate-sale vortex so many years ago and becoming my closest friend forever. (Do not *ever* forget where my journals are, girl!)

To the staff and board of directors at the Village at Manor Park: Tim loved you all so much. Thank you for making him so much a part of your family as he served the residents during his time of service there.

To Alan: thank you for being such an advocate of my husband and the Godly man he was, for standing by my side and assuring me that Tim's life was Manor Park's main concern, for speaking such kindness about him at his Celebration of Life, and for being such a great mentor. Tim loved and respected you so much.

To Donna: thank you for having the courage to make that call. You and Dan were so instrumental in making Midland our home. Thank you, sweet friend.

To the Permian Basin Regional Planning Commission: you were amazing to me, as I walked those first steps and last steps of Tim's journey on earth. Thank you.

To Sue: thank you for standing by my side and never putting anything before my needs. Oh, how Tim loved and respected you as a leader and friend. I will forever be grateful for being allowed to work under such great leadership and being loved by a woman of faith as you are. I passed along the angel you gave me on that very dark night, as we sat in Tim's room, to someone in an ER who was in great need. I shared with that person that you were the giver of the angel and that it was given to always be a protector of those hearts that are grieving. I love you.

To Yadi: thank you for praying by Tim's bedside as you wept and held his hand and for being available to my family as we needed you. Your strong faith in our heavenly Father was so evident and brought such peace. I love you.

To Patty: as you walked your own horrific journey at that time, you loved me and stood by me during those long hospital days. You and Dennis were such sweet friends, and Tim loved how you loved the Lord.

To my sweet Ray: you were such a prayer warrior for me. We spent many hours on the road together, and you allowed me to share my anger, disbelief, and love loss of my sweet Tim. You wept with me, as you loved him so much. You reminded me of his deep, abiding love toward me, as he always said, "Yes, dear," and did all he could to honor me. We spent many hours laughing and shopping in Ross Dress for Less—just a moment or two of joy. Thank you.

To Cindy One: you knew Tim's needs while he was in the hospital and made sure everyone followed the guidelines. Thank you for honoring him at the Ombudsman Volunteer Luncheon. I love you sister.

To Barnie: thank you for sneaking in past the hospital troops and making that mad rush down the hall, with goodies packed high in that hospital bed. What a driver you were and a true friend. You always made me feel appreciated, a very vital part of the Planning Commission, and valuable in what I could add to our mission. Thank you.

To Cindy Two: in spite of my negative attitude about support groups, you put up with me and gently carried me through. I will never forget the night you showed up at my house at bedtime, knowing how difficult it was for me to sleep. You sat on the side of my bed, held my hand, and prayed for me 'til I nodded off. Thanks for letting yourself out that night. Thanks for sharing many Antique Barn days with me and making wonderful memories that allowed me to breathe again.

To my sweet friend Karen: Tim knew you before I did. You were one of those other women in his life whom he loved and respected so much. You were so passionate about serving those thrown into the journey of grief and pain. You also served in many capacities with my many ventures as the Caregiver Program Specialist for the Area Agency on Aging. I could always count on you to be available. And after Tim's death, I remember the day you came into my office, knowing I was about to take off on my wandering trip, and brought me a handmade teddy bear with a white collar and burgundy tie. I will never forget what you said: "This is your Tim bear to carry along with you on your journey, to sit beside you, to remind you of his love for you and the love of the Lord for you." I write about Tim's tweed jacket in this book, and you took that jacket and made two Papa Tim bears for my daughters' homes so that he could be ever present in the lives of my sweet grandchildren. Karen, thank you for your love for me and for Tim.

And then, there are those friends of the olden days, those true-heart friends.

To Rick and Janet: thank you for being in Midland within a few hours after we contacted you with the news of Tim's death. Thank you for wrapping your arms around the girls and letting them know how much you loved them during this time of great loss. You both loved Tim so much; he knew that and loved you so deeply. Rick, you and Tim were a mighty team that led Hendrick Medical Center to the level of care it was. Thank you for believing in him. Thank you for sharing your heart during Tim's Celebration of Life service. Your words were such comfort to the girls and me.

To Monty and Pam, our New Year's Eve buddies: I remember those glasses of fake bubbly, as we laughed and brought in the new year with a great pot of soup. Thank you both for standing by our side during those darkest moments at the hospital. Monty, I will forever be so grateful for your part in preparing Tim's Celebration of Life service with such intricate details about his love for the Lord. I know you and Tim shared many Baylor moments together, but the times the four of us shared together were rich and meaningful. Pam, Doc was one of Tim's favorites, maybe because they had such similar personalities. Enough said.

To Carolyn and Paul: thank you for enriching our lives as newlyweds. Paul, you and Tim were like two guys who could finish each other's sentences, as long as they ended with *ace*. You sold cars, houses, insulation, artwork, oil wells—the list goes on, but you were true buddies. Your letter to me after Tim's death brought me such comfort. I still read it, fourteen years later. Thank you. He loved you so much.

Lots of homemade tostado chips and hot sauce at midnight!

Carolyn, you became my friend before I even knew your face, but I knew your heart. Thank you for loving Tim, supporting us throughout our marriage, loving our children, and being my friend on whom I could always depend when it came to our prayer closet. We have walked many paths together. I will always cherish our friendship. Thank you.

And then there were those who touched our souls through worship and praise.

To Fred and Mindy: we wanted a celebration of Tim's life; you made that happen through music. The words to "I Can Only Imagine" still remain close to my heart. All the music was from the Most High, and Tim loved any worship service that the two of you led. Fred, thanks for reaching out to Casey and Kelly, letting them know of your deep love and support. You helped raise them in the Lord. Thank you.

To Brother Stan, my pastor: I owe so much of my strength in walking through those days of desperation to you. Brother Stan, thank you for the times you ministered to our family as we raised our children, as we grew in the Lord as a family, and as you stood by our side during some of the most wonderful, meaningful times in our lives—and then during the most difficult time in our lives. Thank you for making several trips to Midland to support us and for praying for us in the pulpit on that Easter Sunday morning. When I got off the elevator on April 19 at Zale Lipsey Hospital in Dallas, there you sat in the waiting room, waiting for Casey, Kelly, and me. You will never know what it meant to us that you stood beside us in the room when the doctor told us Tim was heaven-bound. You also were there with us on the day Tim took that walk through the heavenly gates. I remember your words so clearly: "It is good for us to walk those that we love and are heaven-bound through the gates of heaven, when it is possible." You then asked for everyone to share sweet memories about Tim. Those were moments I will never forget. Then, bringing us full circle, as we celebrated his life on April 23, you closed that time at the grave by toasting to Tim Adrian with cold Dr. Peppers, making that expression of our love for our husband and daddy OK. You will always be my pastor.

I realized quickly the importance of having a true friend of Tim's read this book in its entirety, so I immediately turned to Rick Defoore, who agreed to take on this great task for me. He knew Tim in a way that many did not and knew Tim's story. Rick walked many miles with Tim. He and his wife, Janet, shared a multitude of chocolate chip cookies with us— handmade by Tim, thanks to Mimi. But Tim and Rick shared something so much deeper than most—a love for the Lord. That bond was always there and evident in their friendship.

As Rick and I were sharing, he opened my heart to a part of Tim Adrian that many should know. Rick was one of Tim's best friends, but he was also his boss while working for Hendrick Medical Center in Abilene, Texas. What a team they were. Rick told me there were many times he would head out to Mesa Springs, Hendrick Medical Center's retirement community, where Tim was the director, to see Tim. Rick shared a very heartwarming observation:

"Once I arrived at Mesa Spring, I would head to Tim's office. I could rarely find him there, though, as he was always out and about, among the residents and staff, within the community. But often, I would head to the day room, where I would find him kneeling down beside one of the residents' chairs, listening to their stories from their hearts."

Rick, I will forever love you and Janet for your precious friendship.

As I look at all these names—and there are so many more; forgive me for not noting them all, but you know who you are—I see in these people the face of Jesus. This acknowledgment is the most important part of this book, for if it were not for the folks in these chapters of my life, I would not have survived.

My prayer is that this book will be a spiritual guide for you as you search for peace, comfort, joy, and hope again and that it might help you to see the many promises of God during this journey of desperately trying to find a new kind of normal.

These stories from the heart are the source from which I gained my strength to put in writing how very mighty God is. He can be mighty in your journey also. Please open your heart to what He has to say to you. He wants to be your strength, stronghold, and the source of your survival, as He has been mine!

Introduction

I will never forget that exceptionally long, sultry day in St. Louis, Missouri, while I was serving with the Baptist Mission Board as a summer missionary to little children in the inner city, when I received words from my mother's heart.

I had been shattered because of a broken heart, and she had prayed for God to mend the broken pieces. She was a wise woman, a prayer warrior like none other. She knew God had so much life, joy, and peace stored up for me, but she also knew that a broken heart was a physical condition, one that only God could gently put back together.

At the age of eighteen, I had met the love of my life—at least, I thought he was the love of my life. After three years in a somewhat uncertain relationship, my dreams quickly dissipated, like sand running through my fingers, even as I tried to hold on to every grain with every bit of strength I could muster. I honestly thought, *How will I ever be able to trust again, breathe again, pick up the pieces of my life again, and move forward?* I had thought I was walking in God's perfect plan.

When my mother called me on that day, however, the excitement in her voice was something I will never forget.

"Lillian Anne, the man God has been preparing for you since birth has been sleeping in your brother's bedroom all summer. I can hardly wait for you to come home and meet him."

"Mother, please stop matchmaking," I said. I could feel her smile over the phone. She wanted my pain to stop and for me to see clearly. God has our lives in His hands, even when we have doubts.

A few days later, I received a letter in the mail, and I knew that, somehow, my mother had played a part in instigating it. No one could ever say no to Maxine Jolly.

He was serving as a summer missionary with the Baptist Mission Board at my father's little church in Pittsburgh, Pennsylvania, working with the youth of the community for that summer. His summer term ended a week after mine, meaning we would spend a week together after I got home, since he was living in my house. I would become his main mission project!

His letter was gentle, kind, funny, God-filled, and somewhat to the point. He was going to have a Youth Camp to wrap up the summer Bible studies he had been leading all summer, and he wanted to know if I would be a counselor during that weekend at the lake. Of course, I was thrilled to be asked, as serving within my own church was something God had laid on my heart while in St. Louis. To come back and make a difference in the lives of those youth who were starved to know more about God's perfect plan in their lives greatly appealed to me.

Not that I knew what God's plan for me was at the time, but I knew for sure He wanted me to have a servant's heart.

That late-summer morning, when I woke up in my own bed for the first time in almost three months, there was such peace in my heart about being home again. I loved what I had done all summer, touching the lives of many who had no one to show them God's love. Those sweet little children had burned their handprints on my heart forever, but I was ready to be back and ready to serve within my own church.

I grabbed my pink caftan, threw it over my head to cover up my pj's, and walked into the kitchen—and into the arms of my two-year-old nephew. He was sitting in his high chair, waiting for me. He loved me as much as I did him. Missing him was probably the hardest part of my summer. As we snuggled and giggled together—and he got oatmeal all over me—I smiled from the inside out with delight. He was so important in my life and still is.

And then, out of the corner of my eye, I saw a quiet, handsome young fella with auburn hair, wearing a pair of worn-out blue jeans and a white T-shirt. He was barefoot and small in stature, and he was grinning from ear to ear as he watched love in action.

I turned toward him. My mother was sitting in her chair, watching with those I-told-you-so eyes. He stood up, walked across the room, stuck out his hand, and said, "I am so glad to finally meet the love of Nolan's life, Aunt Lilly. My name is Tim. Welcome home."

Oh my, the simple touch of his hand, his smile, the dimples in his cheeks, and that auburn hair—it took my breath away. I knew then that my mother might have something there, and he'd been sleeping in my brother's bedroom all summer.

My question in my heart was, *I wonder what his thoughts are?*

We spent some time together that evening, going over what he wanted me to do for the Youth Camp, and then he did something that I had never experienced with anyone I had ever dated. He reached out his hand and said, "Let's pray for those youth we will be ministering to this weekend." What a sweet moment and one that left me speechless, knowing God did have someone picked out for me who was a true godly man of integrity—and - I might even be staring him in the face. How blessed I felt that very moment.

Not knowing what his heart felt, I immediately prayed for him.

The Youth Camp weekend was amazing. The youth of that old steel-mill town in Beaver County, Pennsylvania, had come together to see God in a true light. The whole weekend was centered around God's amazing grace and His free salvation for all of us who choose.

Late that evening, after all the campers were down for the night, Tim asked me to go for a walk with him down to the lake so we could spend some time in prayer for the next day; it was going to be the day when, we prayed, many decisions would be made for the Lord. Of course, I was eager to do the same.

We walked, talked, and laughed a little. When we came to the edge of the lake, we saw an old, bulky tree limb that had fallen close to the water, and we sat down on it. I took off my flip-flops and wiggled my toes in the water as we spoke of God's love and our responsibility to share that love with each young person in attendance. Tim reached over and took my hand, and we began to pray. God's presence was wrapped around us as we lifted each camper by name.

As we completed our time of prayer and started back to the campsite, the moon and stars shone brilliantly. Tim stopped and turned toward me, saying, "God has impressed upon my heart to kiss you."

No one had ever used that as an excuse to get a kiss from me, but I did not hesitate—I was certainly not going to argue with God. That kiss sealed it in my heart. I knew my mother had a true connection with the Lord, and Tim to be the love of my life. What a sweet moment of healing took place in that simple kiss.

After three years of a long-distance relationship, Tim asked my father for my hand in marriage. I was sitting there when Tim called, and I heard my dad say, "Let me talk to Lilly for a moment." His question to me was, "Do you love him? Love him totally with all your heart, through times of greatness and times of despair? Do you trust him to love you back and always take care of you?"

"Daddy, without a doubt," I said.

I graduated from Southwest Baptist University on May 21, 1977, at noon. At four o'clock on that same day, in the chapel of SWBU, I married the love of my life. Once again, my mother—my friend, my prayer warrior—knew God had me in His hands.

Chapter 1

The Walk of a Widow

The heart is one of the most powerful organs in our bodies. We need it to beat strongly for us to survive.

Love is one of the most powerful emotions. We need it to fulfill the innermost desires of our hearts. Without love in some form, we could not survive the pains of life.

Did you know that a broken heart is a true physical condition? I had identified mine as the flu, but the doctor said, "Nope."

Some call it a broken heart, but it's a genuine physical condition that affects our whole being. It hurts from the front of the chest to the back of the body. It causes memory loss, confusion, suspicion, achiness, wanting seclusion, anger, bitterness, emptiness, doubt, and the desire to no longer exist. How can loving someone so deeply bring about such pain that is immeasurable? That's the pain we describe as a broken heart. It is simple; we love from the heart, and with that comes chance—the chance to experience deep joy, as well as pain that is immeasurable.

We may talk of experiencing a broken heart, but until you have loved and then experienced the loss of the one you loved, you can't begin to realize this deep, inner gnawing pain; the thickness in your throat that makes you feel as though you cannot swallow; the feeling that you will no longer be able to breathe.

To survive the many forms of grief that come with loss, we find that sharing our stories give us strength.

On this long journey called grief, we seek those who know this pain. Sharing our story with others becomes a necessary part of the healing process. And if, by taking this chance and sharing those deepest thoughts, we can touch another person's life, then the pain lessens for us and for them also. Ah, God is so good to allow us joy again.

Please allow me to share my story with you from deep within my heart.

I will share parts of my journals that I kept close to my heart in those first few months after the tragedy of losing my husband.

I will share my story because the search is deep and long and hard, and I have walked it and am still walking it, even fourteen years later. I share my story because the ache and pain need to be shared; I thought I had no one to share it with who really understood. I share my story because of the anger, disbelief, confusion, emptiness, loneliness, abandonment, and ache that hurts from the front of my chest to the back of my body, which, I have learned, is normal. I share my story because as I've tried to dig deep within those broken pieces, trying to figure out how to live again, I've come to the realization that the deeper you love, the deeper the pain.

I will share my story because finding a new kind of normal is a *must*, but it is the hardest part of the grief journey, and I want to walk it with you. Walking a journey with someone who *truly understands* makes it a walk that can be!

The Call

On Sunday evening, April 1, 2007, Tim and I met our friends Pete and Cathy at our favorite Mexican restaurant, Dos Compadres, in Midland. Tim and I had had a somewhat stressful weekend but nothing out of the ordinary; stress came with the territory of flipping houses, and we loved it. Still, I've felt guilt for all these years because I just wanted to get that room finished. Was it my pushing Tim that caused this tragedy?

At the restaurant, Cathy said to Tim, "Are you feeling OK?"

"Sure, why?" he said. "Is this an April Fool's joke question?"

"No, you just look weary," Cathy told him.

Why did I not see that? Was I blind to what was staring me in the face? That moment still haunts me—something Cathy could see, but I could not. We move through life with so many ups and downs, taking each moment for granted, saying, *I can fix this tomorrow*, but then, tomorrow never comes. Not in the form you dreamed it would.

First lesson learned: every moment must be valued. Remember that it is a gift, not a promise.

How do you kiss the love of your life goodbye one morning as you both leave for your normal workday routine without even beginning to realize it's the *last* time you will hear their voice? Life appears to be normal, but the most unbelievable definition of *normal* is about to take place.

It *was* a normal Wednesday morning. But then again, what does normal mean? Tim brought me the last cup of coffee he would ever bring to me. We shared the bathroom, getting ready for work together, for the last time. We talked about who would pick up supper and what it would be—the last time a meal together would ever be discussed. He kissed me goodbye and told me he loved me. It was not the last kiss, as God granted us more of those precious kisses, but it was the last time I ever heard his voice. How would I remember what his voice sounded like? How would I remember his laugh? I did not know I would *have* to remember it. I thought I would always hear it.

Horrors like this only happen to other people, never to me.

The phone rang at my desk as I began my day at work—the call I will never forget; the silence in the air. A familiar voice was on the other end, one of our best friends, who worked with Tim at the Village at Manor Park.

"Hi, Donna. How are you?" I asked.

"Not too good, Lilly. It appears that Tim may have had a small stroke. We have just called 911. They are taking him to Midland Memorial Hospital."

"A *stroke*? I don't understand what you're saying."

She repeated, "We think Tim has had a small stroke, and we're heading to the hospital to meet the ambulance there."

"What hospital?"

"Midland Memorial."

"I am on my way."

I was certain that the person at the switchboard must have tapped through to the wrong phone line, as my husband was the power of strength and health. Besides, this was *our* time—flipping houses, antiquing and junking, Saturday day trips, visits to Dallas to see our kids on a whim,

3

doing all those things we had dreamed of doing but could not do because of having the responsibilities of raising a family and making a living. This was *our time.* Was it possible that call really was for me?

We had only lived in Midland for two years, moving there from Abilene, Texas, where we had raised our children for twenty-eight years of our married life.

We were approaching our thirtieth wedding anniversary on May 21. Many plans had been made for that special anniversary—a cruise, already paid for, and a three-karat diamond ring that I had told Tim had *better* be a part of the celebration. Of course, I gave him a year's notice so there would be no excuses, and he had purchased it for me, but I was not allowed to wear it until the big day.

As I rushed to Midland Memorial Hospital, not even being certain where it was located, I learned quickly that it would become a part of my life for the next several weeks—very long weeks.

I called my mother and Cathy. I had to tell someone what was happening. Cathy immediately called Pete, and he met me at the hospital, not to leave my side for many hours. Pete and Cathy had been our friends for over twenty years.

I got there before the ambulance arrived. I did not know what to expect. All had seemed so normal that morning. All had seemed so normal when we'd gone to bed the night before. In fact, Tim had shared the exciting news that he had just gotten an email, informing him that he had won an award for a paper he had written in his master's degree class at Abilene Christian University. He was the oldest in his class and the wisest; he had the experience the others lacked in dealing with life issues that sometimes throw you a curve ball. That is what his paper was all about. How ironic that he would win the prize when we were about to learn that lesson.

The ambulance finally arrived, and as they wheeled Tim into the ER, I stood in disbelief. He seemed to be searching for me, and when I approached him, I saw that very familiar look in his eyes, as always. I knew he wanted to reassure me that all would be fine, that this was just another hill to climb, but it wasn't one that he could climb for me.

Tim always took care of me. *Never* did I worry or wonder if he could provide for the girls and me.

That "normal" Wednesday morning became a nightmare that I never dreamed would be mine. This sort of thing happened to those folks who live next door, or down the street, or in another country but not to me.

Tim was five foot seven and weighed about 150 pounds. He was as strong as an ox and had never been sick a day in our married life. So how did this happen?

Then I met his doctor, a tall man with a bedside manner that left much to be desired. When he saw that Tim had been intubated, he was none too pleased. He immediately wanted to know *who* gave permission to do that procedure. When the nurses said it had been done as a lifesaving procedure, he again demanded, "Who gave you permission to do this procedure?"

It was not until weeks later that I understood why he was not pleased that the procedure had been done.

The doctor and I had never met prior to that moment, so his next words, after only having just met him, were piercing and still ring in my ears: "Your husband has less than a 50 percent chance of survival. With his blood pressure at 220/140, what he experienced was a massive stroke and a spontaneous intracerebral hemorrhage, which is best described as *worse* than a gunshot wound to the head. *If* he survives, he will never regain more than 30 percent of his normal ability to function." He was abrupt and to the point; I was just another face with another person who needed his care.

At that moment, I felt like I was having an out-of-body experience. *When did the word* massive *appear? I thought it was a* minor *stroke. Now it's massive?*

Pete was in the room with me, incredibly quiet and just listening. Once the doctor left, Pete, working so hard to be strong, walked over to me with tears streaming down his face and said, "Lilly, listen to me. No one but God has the last word, not man. The end of the story has not been revealed."

Pete will never know the hope that gave to that moment of disbelief. God did have the last word. Do we always want his last word, though? Not always, but it is perfect, regardless of how we feel at the moment. Pete reminded me of God's Word being truly clear on this:

> Blessed is the man who remains steadfast under trial, for
> when he has stood the test he will receive the crown of

life, which God has promised to those who love Him. (1 Peter 5:10 ESV)

I found that to be an appropriate scripture, coming from my dear friend.

So what was my next step? My life was falling apart in front of me, and the person who always had the answers during our most stressful times could not speak. I could not ask Tim what to do, or where to turn, or to please help me fix this. He always had the answers; he was the calming factor in our lives; he was our balancing act. Now, I had to make the decisions alone.

Soon, the cool relationship with his doctor would change. He very soon endeared himself to me and Tim. He developed a sense of determination that he would do everything within his power to bring us full circle so that Tim could at least function as best as possible under our dreadful circumstances. He became my best friend.

This would be my new kind of normal, a normal that I had begged God for. I would take any part of Tim that I could get, if I could just get *some* of him back.

There were people all around me, yet I felt so alone. I began making phone calls to his brother, his sister, and his mother and father. It was so hard to tell Mimi that her precious son had very little chance of survival.

I got a call from Cathy, Pete's wife, my dearest friend of all.

She asked, "Have you called the girls?"

"Of course not. I don't want to worry them." I was still in denial that this was massive and not going to go away.

Cathy very calmly said, "Lilly, you need to let them know what is happening; they need to come."

So I made the phone call. The terror and devastation in their cries will be forever embedded in my heart and still ring clearly in my ears. Not their daddy; he was their stronghold. Kelly's first words to me were, "He is not going to die, is he?"

As a mother, of course I said to her, "No, honey, he is not going to die, but it is very serious." I was telling her the truth. The truth that I felt I knew, that we would all survive this nightmare.

Casey wasn't home when I called. Her husband, Damon, later told her only that she needed to contact me. Casey is my child who works inside the box; all lines are very clear, and we just work within those parameters. Kelly is one who works with emotions and has no problem showing them and sharing them. But this time, Casey expressed herself. Her first words were, "No, no, no. This can't be true." Once she calmed down, I shared with her that there was hope, and she immediately kicked into her box form and started making realistic plans.

They both made plans to fly to Midland and begin this journey with me. We had no idea what faced us, but we were willing to do whatever it took to bring healing to our broken hearts.

Seeing Tim for the first time in such a vulnerable state was exceedingly difficult for them.

What had started out as a very normal day for them was never to be again. Not the usual kind of normal. We would never know what that was again. Thus began the journey of three long weeks of grabbing hold of every moment, working hard to find hope—every sign, every bell that rang, every number on the monitors that were to tell Tim's fate.

Chapter 2

My New Kind of Normal

The days to follow were a mere blur to me. I tried so hard to soak in every bit of information the doctors gave me. I realized this was my life, not someone else's, and I needed to absorb as much as I could of my new normal.

I reference my "new kind of normal" quite often in this book. That's because there is nothing of the norm in my life anymore—at least, what I had called normal. I was a wife; now I'm a widow. I had my best friend with me every day; now I'm alone. I am a grandmother but without a grandfather to love with me. I no longer have a witness to my life.

That is the main key to my new kind of normal.

We all want a witness to our lives, our comings and goings, our accomplishments, our struggles. When we have had that as a normal part of our everyday being and then it's gone, we search desperately for a new kind of normal.

Everything in our daily walks changes. Nothing is the same; nothing is routine. It is a void, without meaning, an empty feeling of abandonment. We wander in our own silent grief until we find a new kind of normal; part of that, hopefully, is others who fill that void. Not in the same way but in a new way.

That's the reason we search for a new kind of normal. Hopefully, the biggest part of our new normal is a renewed relationship with our heavenly Father, husband, protector.

That is his desire for our hearts!

Tim's room quickly filled with friends who loved him, from the executive director of the Village at Manor Park, where Tim was the eldercare administrator, to the housekeepers there. They loved Tim so deeply and felt cheated out of the best thing that ever had happened in their lives—someone they trusted; someone who valued them, believed in them, and knew that they could become whatever they wanted to be. He made them realize each day that what they were doing was one of the most important things they could ever do for the folks they were taking care of—giving them a clean home, clean sheets, clean socks, true dignity. These folks were committed to their jobs. Later, throughout those hospital days, I learned that lots of their commitment was because of who believed in them. That was my husband, the kind of man he was, affirming, gentle-spirited, a true godly man of integrity. He was a person who lifted you up when you thought you couldn't walk through the day. He made you smile when you thought you had nothing to smile about, and he constantly affirmed you when you were not sure that what you were doing was meaningful. He did this through simple acts of kindness and many sweet life savers.

Now, this person, a man of godly stature with a true servant's heart, was lying in a bed, vulnerable to those with whom he had served. Was I wrong to allow him to be exposed to the world that loved him in a way they had never known him? That question was quickly answered in my heart as *every* person who visited acted as if they knew that this could be one of their last intimate moments to tell him what he had meant to them and how much they respected him as a leader and a man. I asked them to sign a journal that I was keeping during this time, so that when Tim was going through the worst of physical therapy, I could show him the names of those who believed in him, as he had believed in them, and tell him that they were waiting for him to return to the job set before him. People in his life shared how valuable he was to them.

I specifically remember this journal entry from his sister, Susan:

4/7/07—Saturday

Wow, what an experience thus far. Fear, faith, hope, disbelief, surreal love, and family. All words to describe your ordeal. Memories flood my mind. Hovering over you, I check your breathing (sounds like Mimi), fix your sheets, hold your hand, *pray*, cry, hope, fight the anger of why, and love you. I remember so clearly you answering my questions about Jesus. Thank you for the life we shared as I was growing up. A beautiful influence. As I watch the friends file in and out, I am honored to be your sister. I am praying for you, believing in your every moment. One day soon, we will talk, laugh, and share a Dr. Pepper together.

I love you.
Susan

There were many moments of "how in the world did we get to this point?"

But I never gave a thought, not for a minute, to the possibility that Tim might not survive this medical situation. I was leaning on God's Word, which clearly says, "Ask and you will be given what you ask for, seek and you will find. Knock and the door will be open" (Matthew 7:7 TLB). I was asking, in faith, and believing. I did not think I was in denial, as I am sure many thought I was.

I was *believing*.

Daily, I watched for signs of positive change. And daily, we saw them. His speech therapist would come in and ask him questions using sign language. At one point, she was so excited about his progress that she said to him, verbally, "Mr. Adrian, what month is this?" Of course, there was no sign for "April"; at least, we *thought* there was none. Tim quickly showed us that he could answer this question too, while intubated, as he held up four fingers—the fourth month of the year. He wanted us to know he could communicate well. We were all delighted. We were all seeking hope.

The doctors came and went. We waited for them early in the morning and late in the evenings. Each day, I would ask for a CAT scan. They would oblige, even though they did not think it was necessary. It was the test that daily assured me—at least, I thought it was assurance—that the clot within Tim's brain was reabsorbing itself back into his system and that his chance for survival was increasingly more optimistic.

Now, *survival* to me was breathing, even if he was wheelchair-bound or bed-bound. I begged God for the opportunity to serve Tim as he had served me for so many years. I would take him any way that God chose to give him to me. But *survival*, from a medical standpoint, from a spontaneous intracerebral hemorrhage meant having maybe 30 percent of your mobility back, but even that was a stretch and would be a miracle.

Still, a miracle was what we were waiting for. I knew God would once again use my husband to do something mighty. I never stopped long enough to realize *who* was truly mighty.

As the days passed between April 4 and April 21, we spent time working toward moving forward, whatever that was going to mean. As we sat, day in and day out, in a hospital room, we continued to find ways to communicate with Tim. The girls would bound into the room, saying, "Hi, Daddy," and head to the side of the bed to hold his hand. He would take theirs and raise them to his lips to kiss them.

I will never forget the day he decided to kiss me and not on my hand. No, he aimed for the lips. We were working hard on communicating, me on his right side and the girls on his left. When he could not discern what one of us was saying, he would take my hand and kiss it. Well, this time, he decided to rise out of the bed and kiss my lips. I was afraid to take the side rails down from the bed for fear of pulling a wire or disconnecting something. So I leaned into the bed, and right as he was about to kiss my lips, he began to choke horribly. We just knew he was dying. The girls and I ran out into the hall and screamed, "*Hurry*! He is dying!"

Of course, nurses came running, but by then, Tim had coughed good and was settling back down, doing fine, and looking at me out of the corner of his eyes. I hadn't thought about the tube down his throat, and as he rose up in the bed, the tube pulled him back down. The girls immediately said, "Mama, no more kissing." That was our last attempt toward intimacy.

After the first day or so, Kelly was the one to realize that perhaps some of Tim's confusion was because he wasn't wearing his glasses. When she asked him if he wanted his glasses, his eyes lit up. He wanted to put them on himself, and we allowed him to do that. He was very independent. He wanted to attempt everything himself. He wanted to show us and the world that he would rise above this. He was bound and determined to become strong again. Once those glasses were on, he was a new man. He wanted to open his own mail—with one hand, I might add—get out of bed by himself, and sit up (most of the time, in the middle of the night).

And he genuinely wanted to breathe on his own, but for some reason, this was something he could not do. He had done almost anything I asked him to do throughout our marriage. But I knew we were in serious trouble when we could not get him off that ventilator. Taking deep breaths for him seemed something of the past.

When asked to do so, he would immediately reach over to his left hand and, with his right, wrap his fingers together. With the strength of his right arm, he would lift his left and begin doing arm lifts, sometimes forty repetitions at a time. This was his way of saying, "I am trying, and I *will* get strong again."

Many people came and went. Family, friends, coworkers. Some folks I had never met, and others I knew very well. His coworker Lucy came to visit him; she loved Tim so much. He was sitting up in a chair, and they discussed things such as updates to the rooms and common areas where the residents lived, as they often did. She looked at Tim that morning and said to him, "Wanted you to know—we have decided to paint all the resident's rooms *orange*."

I don't know what the past conversations had been between Lucy and Tim, but I knew *she* knew that comment would bring a little smile and maybe a chuckle to the conversation. Or perhaps even put a little fire under him. She was so right. As he looked her straight in the eyes, he held up his finger and wiggled it back and forth, as if to say, "Oh no, you won't."

She laughed too. They were true buddies. Those were the moments I loved to see.

People came in and prayed for him. Sat by his side and sang to him; read scripture to him. Many came not once but every day. Patty, our next-door neighbor, came often. Patty was going through so much herself. She had recently been blessed with a new granddaughter who had medical issues. Yet Patty was faithful in standing beside me every moment that she could. That is so important during such a time—to have friends who are true friends and will stand beside you.

Sometimes, though, when you have a loss such as this, many of those who you *thought* were your friends don't know how to deal with your loss.

But Patty always let me know in her actions that I would remain close to her heart.

I had the sudden realization that this man, Tim Adrian, was loved and respected by so many. I thought, *So often we do not take the time to realize the blessings we have until they are gone.*

It was the early morning hours of April 15. I had left the hospital to go home and take a quick shower around five thirty. The girls had come to the hospital to relieve me. When I returned, I noticed lots of anxiety in Tim's room. There was an urgency in the air. I asked what was happening and was told that Tim was no longer responding to light. The clot had begun to bleed again, pressing the left side of his brain over the midline, causing severe damage. I was told he needed immediate brain surgery to remove the clot, or he could die within the hour. All decisions were taken from me. He was rushed into surgery, and we ran behind the gurney, signing paperwork as we traveled down that long hallway.

I made phone calls to anyone I knew who was a prayer warrior. Many friends and coworkers gathered in the waiting room. We knew the possibility of his waking up again was slim, but we were still so very hopeful. Our dearest friend Carolyn, from Abilene, was there quickly, once I called. She stayed until late that day, never leaving my side. She loved me and loved Tim so much. She grieved deeply with me but reminded me of the man of faith that Tim was.

Within a few hours, we were told the surgery was over and had been quite a success, as far as removing the clot. But true success would be determined within hours, when they would check if Tim was responding to light again.

That never happened.

For some reason, I still felt like there was hope. I was not at all ready to give up—the machine that kept his breathing steady led me to believe that my husband was still alive.

I made the decision, after forty-eight hours, to transfer him to Zale Lipshy Pavilion–William P. Clements Jr. University Hospital in Dallas, known as one of the best hospitals for young stroke victims. At this point, I knew I needed the *best*. Tim's doctor agreed to release him, as he knew the desires of my heart—to turn every stone to bring my sweet husband back to a full and meaningful life. The girls also supported my decision, although they knew that their daddy had already been delivered into the hands of our Lord. But this part of the journey needed to take place so that I would know I had done all I could do to protect my husband. Thus, this last leg of our journey began.

Chapter 3

Reality Revealed

Tim's body was very still, frail, and pale as we boarded that medical transport plane at the small Midland airport. I had passed this little landing field many times while heading to the YMCA park to walk, never dreaming I would ever board a plane for a reason such as this.

Once again, the normalcy of this day escaped me. What was normal about any of this? Yet it had become the most normal thing to do—to search and turn every stone to find a way to fix this tragedy. That is what a wife and mother does; she fixes things. *That* seemed normal to me.

Once we landed in Dallas and arrived at the hospital, they quickly took Tim to meet his doctor. I headed to the floor that they took him to. There waiting for me as I exited the elevator, was Bro. Stan, our pastor, from Abilene, along with my precious niece Ashley and her son Jackson, who gave me my IDDY name. They were two especially important folks in my life as well as Uncle Tim's. Jackson and Uncle Tim were true buddies. The girls arrived shortly after I did; they had driven both of our cars from Midland to Dallas. We wanted to make sure we would have transportation available to us for the many trips back and forth from rehab, once we got settled. Again, I still hoped that this trip would be one of the most important trips toward healing.

We had been in the waiting room for about an hour when the attending nurse came out to tell us that the doctor was thoroughly examining Tim and would visit with us shortly.

That short time seemed like forever, but then the nurse came back to escort us to Tim's room, and that walk seemed like forever.

The girls and I, along with Brother Stan, entered the room with great anticipation. The sun was shining brightly through the windows of Tim's room. I felt as though our questions were about to be answered and the true miracle for which I had been waiting was about to be revealed.

How can you believe in an almighty God if you don't walk by faith and not by sight? I was not looking on the outside at a man whose lifeless body lay in a comatose state; I was looking on God's promises to us: *ask and ye shall receive.* Hadn't I asked? Hadn't I prayed for my husband? Hadn't I truly trusted God that he was able to heal Tim fully? I remember asking Cathy those questions. I needed assurance that I had done just that. Prayer was the key, and I knew it.

As the doctor entered the room, I thought that he would reveal to us only what the healing process entailed; nothing more. We had even bought Tim new therapy tennis shoes.

The light, however, was about to turn on.

His words still ring in my ears: "I am very sorry to have known you for only these brief moments and to be the bearer of a report such as this, but your husband and father"—he looked at all three of us—"is never going to wake up; nor is he ever going to breathe on his own again. Now, you have a couple of choices." That sounded positive for a moment, but then he said, "We can help you find the very best nursing home for him, and he can stay hooked up to a ventilator and a feeding tube and possibly survive for years."

That is when I began to learn what surviving really was.

"Or you can make the decision to take him off this machine and see if he can breathe on his own, which is my recommendation."

We all stood in amazement.

We were only thirty days from our thirtieth wedding anniversary and had plans for a great cruise—the trip of our dreams—and Tim had bought me that beautiful three-karat diamond ring, a karat for every ten years.

The girls knew what I was thinking. They knew I would want to hang on to him for a little longer so God's miracle could take place. But they gently said to me, "Mama, this is not fair for Daddy. This is not fair to any of us. The pain is too deep to hang on any longer."

All the while, I was thinking, *Is there anything fair about any of this? Please do not talk to me about fairness. Help me to understand fairness while the man I married for life is leaving me way before life is over, in my opinion. And pain—does anyone know what pain is? No one but me!*

We made the decision on April 21 to disconnect all life support. How do you decide this? Now, tell me truly: what is normal about this?

Well, I found it to be the only normal thing to do.

Family arrived; the hours ticked away. Sherry, one of our dearest friends from Abilene, came to be with me that last night. She had gone through so many losses in her life, and she loved me and Tim. She wanted to be whatever I needed her to be that night. What I needed was to know that she cared that much.

Gaynell and Hadley, two of our dearest friends who had lived in Abilene as we raised our children together and now lived in the Dallas area, came to stand by our side. Gaynell was in true form, a person with a servant's heart. She had food delivered to the hospital so that none of us would have to leave. I am not sure I ever thanked her for that, but what a kind and genuine friend she was. (*Thank you Gaynell.*) They loved Tim. We spent many hours over kids' stuff, school stuff, and just-being-us stuff.

Titus, my nephew, called. Titus loved his Uncle Tim. Tim had an endearing nickname for Titus: Frito. Titus knew that Uncle Tim loved him deeply. Weeping like a small child, he begged me not to let Tim go before he arrived. He came in early on Saturday morning and never left my or the girls' side for days.

We had one last visit with the doctor, and I, once again, asked for assurance that there was nothing more to do for the love of my life. *How can I fix this? There has to be something I can do to fix this.*

Once again, he explained the pictures he had shown us of Tim's brain. There was nothing alive; it was just dark, gray matter. All that had made him the amazing man he was had gone—at least, on this earth.

But the man he really was had already walked through the gates of heaven, receiving his rewards for such great things done on earth.

At a little past noon that day, they took him off the ventilator, and we entered the room.

One thing Tim had wanted for the entire time he was in the hospital in Midland was a cup of coffee. The nurse said to us, "Let's give him that cup of coffee now." She sweetly poured a warm cup of coffee and gave me a mouth swab. I soaked the sponge in the coffee and gently swabbed his lips with it. It was one of the sweeter moments we shared, other than the kiss.

The room began to fill with many folks who loved Tim. Friends, family, those who truly knew this man Tim Adrian.

Brother Stan said, "It is very fitting that those of us who loved Tim should usher him through the gates of heaven, when God permits it and places us in this place and at this time together."

So we did.

He asked those in the room to share those moments in their lives when Tim made a difference.

I stood in awe as I listened to their sweet words. I watched with contentment, knowing that I had been blessed for thirty years to be married to a godly man of integrity.

It was a true worship experience.

My nephew Titus stood next to me, along with my girls, on either side of their daddy's bed.

As I was visiting with those in the room, not facing the heart monitor, Titus, my precious nephew, who stood by our side throughout the rest of those very hard days ahead, quickly saw the heart rate change. He turned to me and said, "Aunt Lilly, it's that time."

Tell me what is normal about watching your husband's heartbeat disappear, but for that moment, it was very normal.

I watched as the numbers on the screen slowly went from in the nineties to zero. I stood in disbelief that there was *no* heartbeat. About that time, the doctor came in and took Tim's vital signs. He turned to me and said, "He has expired."

I was speechless. *He has expired*? Sounded like an item in a grocery store that was a little past the sell-by date; so impersonal. He was talking about *my husband*. How could this be? Just three weeks earlier, we were picking out paint colors, texturing the walls, hauling bead board to our car, and talking about what we were going to do with the other house we were buying to fix up and flip. It was *our* time, our time to do all the things we had dreamed about doing at this time in our lives. Like many other parents, we had spent our time raising our children, working hard, and never standing still long enough to enjoy each other. Now that time to enjoy was here, but he was gone. Why, God? What should I have done differently?

Casey quietly said, "In the words of a wise man, 'It is finished.'"

Kelly reached over to her daddy, took his hand, and said, "Goodbye, Daddy. I love you." My heart was completely broken for my girls— *completely* broken. At that moment, their words pierced my heart more than the fact that Tim was gone.

It is finished, but only on this earth, not eternally.

The realization that he was not gone eternally, however, was not something I could comprehend at that moment. He was just *gone* and would not be my partner ever again.

I looked around the room; those who loved us so were weeping.

One by one, they slowly left the room, and there I stood, alone with my husband for the last time. His face had turned toward the window on such a bright, sunny day. I walked to the other side of the bed so I could look deeply into his face one last time. It was amazing to me that it showed no fear. He looked like the empty shell of the man I had loved for over thirty years. This man *was* gone but not forever. He was resting at the feet of Jesus, and there was no doubt in my heart and mind of this.

I called my parents immediately to share the final news of Tim's passing.

This was when my father, who was in the beginning stages of Alzheimer's disease, said to me, "Lillian Anne, Tim is more alive today than he has ever been before. We will all see him again, and what a glorious day that will be."

How profound from a man who had memory loss, but he remembered the things that really mattered and were true. He was speaking from his "sweet spot."

It was final. No more waiting. Just papers to sign and then on to Abilene to plan the funeral.

The girls and I had made this trip with Titus. He loved Casey and Kelly so much, as they did him. The support was as much to them as it was to me to have him with us.

Picking out coffins. The right color. Would he want me to spend that much? Flowers. What's the right book for everyone to sign? Finding that perfect plot.

I was only buying one plot, as there were not two together, at that time, where I wanted him to be—in the prayer garden in Elmwood Cemetery, underneath a big oak tree. But for now, he needed to be there, and with such short notice, this seemed the best place to lay his body to rest. We had lived in Abilene for twenty-eight of our thirty years of marriage. Raised our kids there. Went to church there. And his parents still lived there. This was the right decision for now. Somehow, though, I wanted to make a huge sign that read, "We *will* be buried together someday." It almost felt like I was not being faithful to him, leaving him alone as I moved on with my new normal life.

I made the girls promise me that they would move his body to Buena Vista, Mississippi, where my parents were to be buried, in the family cemetery, someday, so we would lie side by side again. Of course, as time went by, they knew that might change, and it has, but at the time, they told me what I wanted to hear. I did not know what I wanted at this new normal time in my life. I wanted this nightmare to end, and it was never going to happen for me, at least not today. Decisions, decisions, decisions!

What a chapter in my life—the funeral of the love of my life. I wondered if Tim knew he was the love of my life. I carried such guilt, wondering what I could have done differently to show him that.

Planning a funeral or memorial service is a highly personal process, and your decisions will be shaped by your life experiences.

How to honor, remember, and celebrate the life and memory of the person who died is so hard. But it keeps your heart focused on the positives instead of on the negatives about the death, at least for a few days, and that is good.

Providing Dr. Pepper was a *must* at Tim's viewing and funeral. I remember Brother Stan saying, at the graveside, "And Tim would say to us today, it is five o'clock somewhere, so enjoy a Dr. Pepper with me." We had an ice chest filled to overflowing with cold Dr. Peppers at the gravesite and one at the foot of his coffin during his viewing. So many of his friends drank a Dr. Pepper as they laughed, cried, and reminisced about their friend Tim.

A personalized funeral or memorial service reflects the unique life and personality of your loved one. Again, there is no right or wrong way to make this day what you want it to be.

Should it be an open or closed coffin? Decisions such as this seem so senseless in the scope of the day, yet those questions had to be answered.

The room was packed with folks who had come from all times and places in Tim's life to celebrate who he was and the legacy he had left— childhood friends, college friends, adult friends, professional friends, family who loved him very much. There were over one thousand people at the viewing and the funeral. I remember seeing faces but not what they said.

The pall bearers were chosen very carefully—family, special coworkers, those friends who had been through so much with us as we raised our families together.

Tim's best friend, Rick, led the time of remembrances of who the man, Tim Adrian, was because Rick really knew him. He knew all the right words to say—comfort, peace, speaking of this man of integrity.

Tim always said, "I want my funeral to be a praise-and-worship service."

The songs were specifically picked out for a time of praise.

As Mindy looked down at me to sing her solo, she winked at me as if to say, *This is Tim*. She sang "I Can Only Imagine" by Bart Millard, lead singer of the Christian rock band MercyMe.

> I can only imagine what it will be like, when I walk, by your side
> I can only imagine what my eyes will see when your face is before me

That song continues to ring sweetness in my heart, speaking of God's glory. When Tim took his last breath, his face turned toward the window in his room. The sun was shining brightly, and I could see, with my heart-eyes, him walking through those gates of heaven, standing in the Son.

I don't remember much of that day, except that both of my daughters and my precious sons-in-law stood beside me, along with many family members and friends who loved Tim so much. But I do know that a time of praise and worship took place. That is what Tim wanted. His relationship with the Lord was obvious to those he touched daily. This was one part of his life he never hid. He was very bold in his faith.

The funeral was a time of closure. I was not ready for that closure, but did I have another choice? No.

I realized that I needed someone to stand beside me—someone to look from the outside in, someone who had witnessed these last few weeks with me, which had seemed like long, hard years of pain—and to shed another light on it, so that I could move forward.

I needed for someone to show me God's hand and mercy and that He did have a plan.

Thus, Pete and Cathy, once again, stood in the middle of this journey with me.

Their part of the story comes next.

Chapter 4

God's Hand, from the Outside Looking In

Penned by Pete and Cathy Spano

You never know what a day will bring. Usually, they pass by uneventfully, and only after an unwanted event happens do you realize that, many times, *uneventful* is not a bad thing at all. The defining day of this realization happened to me when I received a call from my sister/friend Lilly. She was clearly distraught, yet calm, and she shared with me the new normal we were about to experience together.

"Cathy, something has happened to Tim. They think he has had a stroke, and he is on his way to Midland Hospital."

With my heart pounding, I assured her we would be there as quickly as possible. Calling Pete was my first step in this journey, as I could not leave my office, and he had flexibility. He immediately left his office and within a moment's time, we were heading into a journey that we never thought, not in a million years, was ahead of us.

This scripture—"I have said these things to you, that in me you may have peace. In the world you have tribulation. But take heart, I have overcome the world" (John 16:33 NIV)—rang clearly in my heart as I realized the significance of his Word and truth.

Our journey in our true friendship with the Adrians began years ago.

Lilly and I both had young girls and met at a Mother's Day Out program. I knew very few people in Abilene, and Lilly, being Lilly, was a people-gatherer, and she invited me to join her and some other girls on an antiques adventure. That was the day my family entered the Adrian vortex of antiquing. Unbeknownst to us, that was the beginning of a lifelong friendship, not just with Lilly and me but with our husbands as well. You know without a doubt that you have been blessed by the Lord when you have couple friendships in which even the husbands like each other, and that is what we had. We raised our girls together, prayed together, supported each other in hard times and in good times, and even were Brownie moms together, having one of the most successful Girl Scout cookie programs in our territory, with many wild twists and turns and loads of fun. We always believed that we would all end our days in Abilene.

As the years passed, God's plans for us all changed, but never did things waver in our friendship.

Tim was offered a job in Midland, Texas. Although saddened by their move, I always felt this move was ordained by God and would be used in a way we had never dreamed. One Sunday morning, I felt I heard the Lord say to me that Pete and I would be moving to Midland. I called Tim and Lilly that morning and asked how they liked it there, and Lilly said, "You're not going to believe this, but I had a dream that you and Pete moved here." Again, God's Word was noticeably clear to me, as He says in Proverbs 16:9, "In their hearts, humans plan their course, but the Lord establishes their steps" (NIV). Our steps were being established in ways unimaginable.

In January, Pete and I made our move to a time in our lives that was richer than *rich* can ever be described. We lived with Tim and Lilly until our house sold. What a wonderful time—we had coffee in the morning together and dinner at night. We had much laughter and true adventure together. Once we sold our home in Abilene, Pete and I move to Odessa, where his job was. Since we had already established a church fellowship together with Tim and Lilly, in between Midland and Odessa, we would meet on Sunday for church—sometimes a little early, and we'd go to breakfast; sometimes after church, and we'd head to lunch. It was as if we just picked up where we had left off in Abilene.

One thing that God showed me during this time in our lives was that we need our Christian brothers and sisters in the Lord to survive the new normals we encounter. It is those God-given relationships that last a lifetime, those on whom we can depend, those who stick closer than a brother or sister. All four of us learned this quickly. "One who has unreliable friends soon comes to ruin, but there is a friend who sticks closer than a brother" (Proverbs 18:24 NIV).

Learning from each other was part of our joy in this friendship. We were always there, available and ready to serve. Tim and Pete were like brothers who, at times, ended each other's sentences. Many times, Lilly and I would walk away, hoping that no one knew that we knew them. They were always into something that we were not sure we wanted to be a part of. And trust me—negotiations were always a part of the moment, from estate-sale Christmas lights to Dillard's end-of-the-year Christmas tree sale, or perhaps a building contractor adding to their new venture. It was nothing for Tim to come home from work and find that Lilly had sold their home. "I mean, why not? We made money off of it." He would just smile, sometimes roll his eyes, call Pete, and say, "Hey, I need a mover." And once again, they would shuffle furniture from one house to the next.

On this particular Sunday, the four of us met for dinner, and only the Lord knows why, but I looked at Tim and asked him if he was OK. I didn't know that would be the last conversation I would ever have with him where he could talk. Tim Adrian was a small-framed man, but I always thought of him like David. There was never a Goliath who Tim was afraid to take on. He was a man of great integrity, a man who loved Jesus with all his heart, and loved Lilly and the girls with everything in him. He was a friend to all. He lived a Christian walk with action, not just words.

I often wonder if Tim did not give up his life for his fellow man. He helped Pete and me move our furniture from a horrible apartment to our little duplex, which would, unbeknownst to us at the time, become the home of his widow for a season. I would ask myself many times if his moving our furniture put too much pressure on Tim, making him a ticking time bomb.

So many questions you ask. *Why* did I ask him if he was OK? *Why* did I notice something different in his look? I would have a lot of whys during this time, as did Lilly, searching for the *whats*. I knew God's plan was always perfect, but understanding it was a real problem for me at the time.

The call, that deep, dark message—why?

I will never forget walking into that room that would become our sanctuary of prayer. Tim was sitting up and gave us the thumbs-up sign.

I was so relieved and hopeful. I thought, *OK, we must put on our prayer-warrior clothes and hit the floor, interceding for Tim and Lilly. Tim will be victorious over this situation. We will all help and do whatever it takes to get Tim back in shape, and this will just be a small challenge, just a mere speed bump, but we will overcome this crisis with the help of almighty God, and Tim will recover.* We left the hospital that night, full of hope and faith. Again, God's Word was revealed to me, and it seemed clear:

> First, then, I urge that entreaties and prayers, petitions and thanksgivings be made on behalf of all men. (1 Timothy 2:1 NAS)

The following were my thoughts and prayers that first night. I was convinced of this outcome:

Lord we are only in our early fifties. How is this happening? Lord Jesus, Tim is one of Your true servants. He is a true bearer of Your truth and light. We just know that he will pull through this with Your help. We just know it. Lilly knows it. She is willing to do anything and everything to help Tim, and we are willing to help them. This must be why you moved us to the same area after living in Abilene so long, Lord. This is the why—we were needed to help Tim and Lilly, as they have helped us on so many occasions. Yes, he will make it, and this is why we are here, as we never thought we would leave Abilene. So this makes sense. Tim will survive this. Thank You, Lord. We believe in Tim's healing. Again, God's Word was revealed. "All the believers were one in heart and mind. No one claimed that any of their possessions was their own, but they shared everything they had" (Acts 4:32 NIV). We were about to share all that we could muster up to be a part of the healing process of this new kind of normal that we were about to walk. But the part we did not know or understand was that we were about to share all of his hope and faith that he gives during a time such as this.

You never know what just one more day will bring. The next day, we saw a decline in Tim. Again, I questioned. I was so upset. I tried to keep a calm face for Lilly, but it was extremely hard. It was hard to see the decline in Tim and still try to maintain a stance of faith. Why, why, why? How many times does this happen in one's life? I kept telling myself that we walk by faith and not sight, so I was going to continue to look to the Lord and pray for healing. That's what Tim and Lilly would do for me, if the circumstances were reversed.

Lilly is a grand planner, and the planner in her kicked into gear. Tim would have shaken his head and laughed if he could have seen her. He had seen the planner in his wife for years. It is one of her gifts to the world; it is how God uses her. So she was planning Tim's recovery. I jumped on the plan with her; it was my greatest hope for Tim and for all of us.

The next days would prove harder than I ever could have imagined. The decision would be made for Tim to have surgery. As we went into the that room one last time and saw Tim's frail, still body, I knew that Tim had left his body, but his body was still alive. Tim was there, but his spirit was no longer there. I was grief stricken. I told the Lord, "You raised up Lazareth; please raise Tim." This was my new prayer.

That night, Pete and I were driving back to Odessa from the hospital, and I reluctantly told Pete, "I do not want to sound like I have no faith, but Pete, Tim is no longer in his body."

Pete quickly said, "Cathy, don't tell anyone else, as we are to walk in his faith."

"Of course I won't," I said. "I'm still praying for healing and for God to send him back to us"—but my spirit told me differently.

The following night, we were at the hospital, having our nightly time of supporting Lilly and her planning, which was still in full force.

"We're taking Tim to Dallas," she said with confidence. There, his fate would be revealed and healing would begin. Lilly left the room for a while, and it was just Casey and me, Tim and Lilly's older daughter.

She looked at me and said, "Cathy, I know that *you* know that my dad is no longer in that body. I know you know this. I'm OK to let my dad go to his great reward because I know he is receiving it, and I'm happy for him. I will forever miss him, but I'm excited at what he is receiving. Just why are we doing all this when you and I both know he is no longer with us?"

With tears streaming down my face, I said, "Yes, I do know he has left us, but we're doing this for your mother. It's what your dad would want us to do. She needs to know that she has exhausted all avenues to help your dad, and we're going to help her through this." So that is what we all did.

Lilly made the call she never wanted to make, and she told us that on a Saturday, we would all gather at the hospital in Dallas, and they would disconnect Tim from life support. *How in the world*, I thought, *can this be normal?* The realization hit me, as I was still hoping and praying that God would send Tim back to us, that it was not to be!

We gathered around his bed and told "Tim stories." So many were of the blessing he had been to many of us over our years of friendship. Much of it was funny stories; much of it was warm and spiritual moments we shared; it was all wonderful. As I listened, I wondered how we could be standing there, laughing and expressing joy for Tim's life, knowing that in just a few minutes, the doctor would disconnect that machine that was giving him life.

Tim's small-framed body soon stopped breathing, and it was finished; at least, on earth it was finished. Ah, then it was clear; it was not a machine giving Tim life. It was Jesus Christ who gave Tim life. And it was abundant still.

Yet the grief and pain for those of us who were left was deep.

The stark reality of his death appeared to be a mere dream. *Surely this is a dream.* We went to Casey's, and the girls decided they needed haircuts before the funeral. I was in disbelief that we were in the Galleria, getting haircuts.

Lilly stopped me in the middle of all the people there and said, "Look at them, Cathy. They don't even know that my world, as I knew it, just ended. They are just walking around, laughing and carrying on, not knowing they walk among people who are hurting deeply with such great loss."

That statement would ring in my ears for days and years and even still does now.

We got back to Casey's, and Lilly and I sat in the backyard. Her little niece came over to her, wrapped her arms around Lilly, and gave her a pin of angel's wings. And at exactly that same moment, I knew that something supernatural had happened to Lilly. A small gust of wind blew across our faces. A large willow tree that sat on the edge of the patio leaned its soft, gentle branches toward her, as if to wrap itself around her entire being, as a symbol of God's almighty protection.

When her niece left, Lilly said, "Cathy, you're not going to believe this, but I just had an angel embrace me in his wings."

"Lilly, I totally believe it. I know it happened, as I just witnessed it."

God had given her such a gift, right at the very moment when she needed it, as our heavenly Father is so faithful to do for us at just the right time.

God allowed a friendship that began at the steps of a daycare center when our children were little. We grew together, we laughed together, we loved together, and we wept together. But it was God's great grace that brought us together for a reason and a season.

I knew God had a plan, although what that plan was, I did not know. But I knew He was almighty. He is what brought us through the journey from loss to life. And I was blessed to be a witness, from the outside looking in.

> For we are God's handiwork, created in Christ Jesus to do good works, which God prepared in advance for us to do. (Ephesians 2:10 ESV)

Thank You, Lord Jesus.

Chapter 5

Lord, Where Are You Calling Me?

The Prayer of This Widow

Today, Lord, I stand before You, seeking Your purpose for my life again.

I want to see a divine purpose in what these new turns in the road of my life mean. It is only through You that I can gain acceptance of a tragedy such as this.

I want to become intentional in listening for Your voice.

I come to You, seeking to feel Your love surround me, like a blanket covers a child, for comfort and security, relieving me of this pain that aches from the front to the back of my entire body.

I want to take the pain and allow it to help me recognize Your desire for me, to hear You through this journey.

Lord, the Bible says You are my husband. As my earthly husband once protected me, I ask for Your protection from all that is unknown.

I know that fear is not of You; please take the fear from my heart.

I am asking for a renewed spirit and hope in You and life itself.

I am asking that joy and peace become real to me once again.

I want the joys that were once there, that are still there, to become once again joyful.

I am asking for peace that surpasses all understanding.

Lord, help me clearly see Your path, and where I cannot see, give me faith.

Allow me to want Your will to be mine in my life. Father, I adore You. I bring my life before You. Oh, how I love You so. Amen and amen.

Chapter 6

The Real Journey Begins

I had finally begun to realize what a New Kind of Normal really was—life without the love of my life. Three weeks in the hospital. Those last moments of a heartbeat. The funeral. Leaving him at a resting place, a place for me to come to but not where he is.

The girls immediately took his clothes from the closet. No questions were asked, and I was in such a new spot in my life that I did not realize much of what was happening. It was genuinely like an out-of-body experience.

Once they went back home to their new normal, I was left to pick up the pieces of my life and put them back together so I could breathe again. Would I ever learn how to breathe again? Would the thickness in my throat ever go away? The bitterness—oh, the bitterness and anger. How do you praise God for taking the love of your life? Did He really expect me to praise Him for that?

One thing I begged God for was to have one last conversation with Tim. We never got to talk again after the stroke, and I wanted to hear his voice. It was storming as I drove toward Odessa that night to stay with our dearest friends, Pete and Cathy. As the rain beat against my car, I cried out to the Lord, "Please, Father, just let me hear his voice one more time."

I got to Pete and Cathy's; they were waiting to embrace me. I truly could not have survived without them. Sometimes, your old friends become strangers to you. No one really knows what to say or what to do, so they often do nothing. That is what happened in my case, with the exception of a few of our closest friends. The pain and silence was almost more than I could bear, but Pete and Cathy *never* let me sit in silence. They prayed with me and read scripture of God's wonderful promises of love unfailing. They wept with me and were angry with me. They never left me alone. They were what I needed—someone to truly be real with me, to not pretend but to let me feel my pain, as they felt it with me. They let me be angry with God and didn't ridicule me. They loved me through the entire process. They loved Tim so much; they too were hurting deeply. I remembered the comment Pete made in the hospital on that horrible day: "Remember, Lilly, God has the last word. Don't listen to men."

I said to Pete that night, as Cathy listened and embraced me, "Pete, was *this* God's will—that Tim should die? Was this His last word?"

Pete's response was clear. "Lilly, we will never understand it all, not until we sit where Tim is sitting. But I can promise you, my sister, that God did get the last word, and we must walk by faith and not by sight. He will be there to pick us up and show us His mercy and grace."

That was hard to swallow. I certainly did not believe it at the time. But you know what? God *knew* I wouldn't believe it at that time, or He just gently loved me through it.

The next day, I went back to our house in Midland, still yearning for that one last conversation. As I was searching through Tim's papers from work, I came across a typed letter—the paper was yellowed, as it had been written years ago. Strangely enough, it was wedged in with papers from Tim's recent days as the eldercare administrator of the Village at Manor Park in Midland.

As I opened this letter, not knowing its contents, I immediately realized this *was* my conversation with Tim. With tears running down my face, I sat in disbelief that I would find this letter at this time. It was addressed to me and went something like this:

Dear Lilly,

Please know how much I love you but how much even more your heavenly Father loves you. I know you are walking through territory right now that you have never

walked before, but know this: that I love you, God loves
you, and we will be together forever!

Love,
Tim

There was much more in that letter, but this is what mattered the most.
I have no idea when or where we were in life when Tim wrote this letter,
but this I *do* know: God was faithful to hear my cry, and He honored my
request to let me hear from Tim one more time.

The Journey Now Begins

But I don't want to be a widow. I don't want to face tomorrow. I don't
want to learn how to start a lawn mower, or plant flower gardens, or choose
paint colors by myself. I don't want to come home on Friday evening after
work and go to the grocery store alone, go to estate sales alone, or get up
on Sunday morning and go to church by myself. I don't want to make a
pot of coffee and drink it alone or look at houses and dream about how to
"make money on this one—alone!

Tim always got home about eight o'clock every evening, I always got
home before him, so coming home to an empty house was nothing new for
me. It was waiting for the door to open, waiting for him to walk in and say,
"Hey, honey, how was your day?" It was getting that call from him before
he came home to ask, "What do you want me to pick up for supper?"—I
rarely cooked anymore; we just did what we wanted to do. That was our
new kind of normal.

What was normal about eating alone after thirty years or pulling those
covers back on the bed and crawling into bed alone after thirty years? The
first night after I came back from Abilene after the funeral, I took a hot
bath. The girls and their husbands were still with me. I got into my pj's
and walked into my bedroom for the first time to crawl under those covers.
Both of the girls walked into the room about that time and crawled in with
me. They wrapped their arms around me, and I fell asleep. They worked
so hard to understand the emptiness I felt. They wanted to be my tower
of strength; they wanted to help me find a new normal, but no one—and

I mean, *no one*—can do that for you. You must do it yourself and only by the grace of God.

My girls knew I would need help walking this journey called widowhood. Of course, I thought I didn't need help I did not want help. I wanted the world to leave me alone and let me learn to breathe again.

Kelly made the first call to their church in Dallas, Park Cities Baptist Church. She told them her daddy had died and that she needed help. They connected her with a lady named Verdell Davis, whose husband had died many years earlier in a horrible plane crash, which took not only his life but the lives of several men they had loved together, for years, as a couple. She wrote a book on this tragedy, *Let Me Grieve but Not Forever*. The church sent Kelly, Casey, and me a copy of this book and one to my best friend, Cathy, so she too could help me as I began this journey.

Kelly visited with Verdell, and Verdell agreed to visit with me, so I made a trip to Dallas to meet this lady who would become one of the most instrumental women in my life from that point forward, helping me to see God's love and almightiness.

I made an appointment to visit with her in her home. She graciously opened her heart to me, and even though it had been years since the loss of her precious husband, and she had married another godly man of integrity, we sat in her sunroom, a place of solace for me for that moment, and we wept together. At that moment, I realized that when you love deeply, the pain of that loss is even deeper.

Verdell invited me to a grief seminar she was doing in Rockwall, Texas, that July 2007. It was held in the home of a woman who had also lost her husband but who wanted to minister to others by opening her home to those who were grieving.

I flew to Dallas for this meeting, not knowing what I would encounter but knowing I needed help.

As I walked into her house, there sat a room filled with young women who had lost their husbands. I thought, *Did any of them love their husbands the way I loved mine?*

As I sat and listened, saying nothing and trying to be invisible in this room, one of the things that Verdell said was, "Do you *want* to find joy again? Do you *want* to continue to feel this pain?"

Before I could think, the words were out of my mouth. "*Yes*, I want to feel the pain. The pain is the only thing I have left to make me feel *Tim*."

The room got quiet; I was certain they hadn't even realized I was there.

I associated pain with Tim. I was afraid that once I felt less pain, he would escape my being, and I did not want to lose that last bit of him, regardless of how painful it was.

"How do I keep him close to me, yet move forward?" I asked.

She gently said to me, "You never let go of those sweet, precious memories. You build on them with new memories."

This was going to be my new kind of normal—building on the old and making my life new.

So often women, feel it is a betrayal to let go of the pain, so they hang on for dear life, rejecting suggestions of ways they can honor their spouses and those sweet memories, yet still begin to rebuild their lives.

I spent a gut-wrenching time in Dallas. As I boarded the plane for Midland, I knew that this would be a painful reminder to me of the last flight I'd taken home to Midland, back in February, when Tim had picked me up after a visit to my sister's for a long weekend. He would not be there this time. How would I walk down that corridor, knowing I was going home alone this time? No open arms to welcome me; no trip to Dos Compadres for dinner after I landed.

As I boarded the plane, I had two choices of seating: one was next to a mother with a wiggling two-year-old who was crawling all over the seating area, chewing on Cheerios and drinking apple juice. The other was next to a sweet, innocent-looking woman who was staring out the window, appearing to mind her own business. Well, I knew I was not up to Cheerios and apple juice, so I chose the sweet lady, sitting alone.

As I settled in next to her, I realized that even though she had appeared to be the kind to mind her own business, she was very eager to visit, and *that* was certainly the last thing I wanted to do. I longed for Cheerios and apple juice at that point. As she began to chatter away at me, I decided the only way I would escape a trip of nonsense, in my opinion, was to pretend I was asleep. I quickly put my things under my seat, buckled in, and began the longest fifty-minute trip of my life.

She was relentless as she tried hard to get my attention. She would tap me on the shoulder and say something, "Oh, ah, hm. I guess she is asleep."

In a few minutes, I once again could feel her breath on my neck; she so desperately wanted to share her thoughts with me, but I did not want to share even a *moment* with her.

As we began our descent into the Midland International Airport, I heard the pilot say, "Ladies and gentlemen, thank you for joining us on this short trip from Dallas to Midland. The weather has been a little rainy, but now it's a beautiful sunshiny day at the Midland International Airport. Please keep your seat belts buckled until we pull up into the boarding area. Again, thanks for flying Southwest Airlines."

As I moved around a little, still wanting to be overly cautious, I bent down to pick up my purse and carry-on luggage, so I could escape quickly.

But this sweet lady sitting next to me was bound and determined that I was not going to miss the joy she had to share. She quickly turned to me and said, "Oh, I am *so* glad you finally woke up. You almost missed the most beautiful sky-filled landscape I have ever seen." Then she pointed out the window to something she had tried desperately to share with me for over fifty minutes—it was the most amazing rainbow I had ever seen.

I was so overwhelmed with what I had almost missed that I began to weep, and I told her my story of loss and how I had begged God to show me rainbows as a symbol of His promise to protect me and comfort me through this time of grief.

She was so kind to me; she reached over and wrapped her arms around me and said, "Well, honey, let me just say to you: always keep your eyes and heart open to God's promises, as He has many to show you."

I found myself constantly searching for those promises. I needed to talk to Tim. I needed to commune with God. I needed to see His hand all over my pain as He journeyed with me.

I searched for tools of the trade, so to speak. I had heard many talk about writing love letters to the one you lost, journaling those deep feelings that you could not express to anyone else.

So, my journaling process began.

I personally found journaling to be very therapeutic for my healing. Also, due to that deep yearning to continue my communication with Tim, those letters in my journal were my way of fulfilling that need.

Many shy away from journaling because they do not know how to put their thoughts on paper. Let me just say this: you put them on paper the way you speak them—at least, that's how I did it and continue to do so.

Let me share with you a few of my journal entries. I journaled like someone who was afraid this would be the last opportunity to ever put her feelings on paper. During a serious conversation I had with Cathy one day, I said to her, "Please, *please* make sure you find my journals when I am gone so that my children don't find them first. They would be so disappointed in me if they saw my innermost feelings." As I had shared the good, the bad, and the ugly with Cathy, we had a sister pact, and she promised me that she would jump to find the journals before anyone else did. It's good to always have a "Cathy" in your life.

I write like I talk, and that's the beauty of journaling. You don't have to use a period or exclamation point or question mark. There never has to be an ending to your sentence, if you don't want there to be. As long as you understand it in the moment you are writing it, that's all that matters. I have gone back into many of my journals and, quiet honestly, I could not even begin to tell you what I was thinking or saying at the time. But that is OK, as I needed it then, not necessarily now. (*Note: I've slightly edited the journal passages below so that they are more easily understandable for readers.*)

Journal 1—Trust in the Lord

4/8—Today is Easter. We started this journey 3 days ago. Hmm, He was crucified, and 3 days later, He arose!

CAT scan comes back. Clot has gone down. The doctor calls it a miracle. I say yes—hundreds are praying.

4/9—lots of folks came by to visit. We are working hard to get you to breathe deep—no luck. You refuse to oblige me on this one; you normally do almost anything I ask by saying, "Yes, dear," but not this time.

Another CAT scan about the same time; PT, OT, and ST begin. You write your name. Tell me you love me in sign language. We begin the process of getting transferred to Baylor. Alan comes by. Tells me of a lady named Connie. Her husband had a stroke and fully recovered; is now dean of the Business School at UTPB. Same kind as yours; brings hope.

4/10—Brother Stan drives in from Abilene. Spends about 4 hours with us, visiting with you and us and those who enter. Such a strength.

A terribly busy day. The doctor thinks you are improving—clot appears to be shrinking. Thank You, Lord, from where all blessings come. Still cannot get you to breathe deep; cannot take vent off until you do.

4/11—Lots of visitors today. You seem so tired. Your mom, dad, brother, and sister come. I put a sign on door, "family only." You needed your rest.

We talked late last night. I asked if you wanted to still buy the house on Story with Kale. You gave a thumbs-up. You signed a POA for me to make decision about house.

Casey got paperwork drawn up; all was signed. Deal done.

I told Kale I was going to want to move us back into that house on Story, where you had so many friends; that it would be good for your healing. Did he want me to buy the house alone without him? His answer was, "No, Tim is our priority. You live there if you want or need. We will cross each bridge each day as it comes."

We now have a house on Story again. Another full day. Still working on deep breathing.

Journal 2

4/27—The Lord is my Shepherd. Those words, I *want* to believe and trust.

5/22—The pain of your death is still deep within my heart. I have walked the first anniversary alone so there is peace that I can do this, but I still do not want to. The question "why" is still there. The difference in the question now is I knew that you knew why, Lord, and that I must just trust. Lord, do You know what a hard task You have given me? I will wait, trust, and see.

5/24—Today empty, lonely; I am exhausted. So many more days like today ahead of me! Lord, why was I chosen to be alone? I go back to worthiness. Hmmm, I was not worthy!

How do you squeeze blood out of a turnip? Paycheck—$1,006.

Bills paid. I am left with $86 until the next payday. Groceries last pay $42; this pay $28. Food that is not good for me to eat; comfort food.

My weight—I am bigger than I have ever been. Each morning I say, Today I will care about me. But I do not care. I have nothing to wear, nothing fits. My skin feels dry, my hair needs coloring, and the cut on my knee is killing me. The house is so quiet. It is Friday. Everyone else is out, busy on this beautiful Friday evening. It is 80 degrees and beautiful outside. I hear the sounds of children laughing, dogs barking, wind blowing, but I'm invisible to anyone, inside my newly remodeled house, with the biggest clothes on that I can find, eating cherry pie, breathing deep, waiting for the sun to go down so that I know for sure no one will come to the door. Of course, I'm only kidding myself to think someone would. I could go to the widows' group supper club, but like Kelly said, I choose not to. Right; my choice, not yours. Actually, sometimes the group (most of the time, in fact) is a reminder to me that I am a widow. I hate that word. Just yesterday, I was married. What happened?

Journal 3

5/25—My precious Tim—my journey begins today, searching for rainbows, promises, answers for tomorrow. Where am I going, Lord?

Can I please, please feel him, Lord? If only for a moment through a rainbow. Midland is behind me for the moment. As I sit where your body lies, the vase is still there. Thank You, Lord. I replace the shocking-pink roses from the girls for our anniversary with rich red ones—deep red for my deep love for you, deep red for the blood shed for us both because He does love me and will protect me and will guide me as I journey to see what lies in front of me, as I seek Him. I miss you. The pain of that void is deeper than imaginable! If I could only see a rainbow. I made it to Dallas, with it raining all the way.

I stopped by your parents' before I left Abilene. Just felt I needed to but only for a moment, and that moment turned into hours. Your mother and father wanted to go to the grave. I was happy to take them. They are hurting so deeply. Your precious mother. Never should a child die before his parents. God help me to be sensitive to them over these next however long!

I took them back home and went back to the grave one last moment. I saw a man searching. I stopped to see if I could help him. He smiled and said, "No, thank you. I spend lots of time out here. More friends living here than I have anywhere else." I told him I had I had just buried my best friend, my husband. You were my best friend, Tim; that is why I am grieving so deeply.

He told me he had buried his best friend twelve years ago. I asked him if it still hurt and if he still missed her, and he said, "Oh yes, and I will always miss her, but we live in a world of memories, and that is why we are able to make it through and gain our joy, but it will always hurt, just in a different way." Hmmm, wonder what that means. I asked him, "Do you ever wish you had made a memory where you did not." He said, "Oh yes, but you cannot live life that way. You live with the memories you have, not the ones you don't have. I always tell my grandkids, always make good memories."

Tim, I'm sorry for not always making good memories for us. But for the good memories, and there are many, thank you. He asked me your name. I told him. He said, "Oh yes, good man. Particularly good man. I am sorry for your loss. God bless you."

I am so glad I took a moment to stop long enough to listen about the blessing of memories.

5/28—Monday, Memorial Day. I left at 7:45 this morning, heading to Mama and Daddy's. I've been there before without you but never because I had no choice. My heart aches. Emptiness prevails, a loneliness that cannot be described. The question again, why? Will I ever get an answer?

My tears cannot stop. My sister said to me just a few days ago, "Remember this, Lilly: when you cry, with every tear that drops, Tim is praying for you."

Big trucks, traffic, McDonald's coffee, filling the gas tank. None of this have I ever had to do alone. I am so sorry I did not take advantage of every moment I had with you. And they were but moments, it seems.

5/30—Sitting on the old back porch. Cloudy. They desperately need rain in this old town. It is so very still and quiet. Nothing moving but the pain in my heart. God's Word says in Hebrews, I believe Hebrews 12, in fact, that you are a part of a host of witnesses, cheering me on! Now I may have interpreted that in the Lilly version. I need to hear you with my own ears, though. Titus called and told me he had a dream about you last night and that you called him by his name, not by Frito, so he knew you were serious. You told him clearly that everything would be all right. He said you had an "Uncle Tim" smile. Several folks who love you have told me they have seen you in dreams, but I have not, and I so desperately want to. I have seen you in letters and through little notes I have found that you had scribbled out to remind yourself of something, but I need to see *you.*

Wow, it is pouring down rain now. Thank You, Lord, oh how they needed this rain in this old Mississippi town. And to think I had just asked You to talk to the Lord about the rain that was so desperately needed.

Tim, I see you. I see you. I see a rainbow, one of God's promises to care for us always. Ah, thank You, Lord, thank You.

6/6—My God. My God, I did not bargain for this. Why, why? No good reason. I am so sad I can't even describe the pain. Help me, Jesus. Help me catch my breath. I cannot carry this pain, this ache in my chest. *Please* help me. I am dying inside. *Help me, help me, help me. Can't You bring him back to me? Please, I've got to have him. If You are the mighty miracle man, then do this, Jesus. Why? Please please!*

No rainbows. No promises. Total darkness. Emptiness. Unbearable loneliness! God, I beg You, please wake me up! This can't be real; it can't be. It can't be. He was so healthy, so strong, *why, why, why?*

It is my sins, I know. How could You be so unmerciful, God? How could You?!

That was one of my strongest journal entries. I haven't shared it exactly as it was written in my journal, but it was one of the most painful moments I can remember. And then there are those entries about lack of trust and suspicion. Let me just say that death is so painful. I never worried about infidelity. Tim was so faithful to me, but once he was dead, lots of doubts came about how faithful he really was. *Is that why God took you so it never had to be revealed?*

My mind was so twisted and torn over this tragedy.

Not trusting God—that was very much a part of my deep grief. After all, His Word says, "Ask and it will be given to you."

Then what in the world happened? That is where Satan loves to move—in doubt. Did I pray enough? Was I faithful enough in my service to the Lord? *There ya go again, trying to earn those work points.* But you know what? God is such a loving God. Never does He turn His back, as we do Him. I, of course, have many more journal entries, and one of them is seeking His forgiveness for my doubt and ugliness, but I just feel His smile and know that I was forgiven before I even asked.

Journaling, such a great tool.

Chapter 7

Aloneness, the Next Step

What a long and lonely summer. Hot, dry. Midland, Texas, but I wanted to be nowhere else.

But as the weekends came, oh, how long they were. I longed for Mondays to arrive again. Yet every Saturday morning, I would get up, take a warm shower, put on a pair of jeans and an old T-shirt, grab my journal, and head to the doughnut shop for a cup of coffee and two doughnuts— one glazed and one chocolate. I had started every Saturday morning for the last thirty years with Tim and a cup of coffee and a doughnut.

I was still living with Pete and Cathy, as the new *old* home I had bought was being gutted and remodeled. I knew Pete and Cathy loved me—everyone needs a Pete and Cathy in their lives—but I also felt strongly that I needed to be absent on weekends as much as possible so that they could find some normalcy in their lives with the new addition to their family—me. Abilene was a little over two hours away, but once I checked on the construction team at the house, I would journey to Abilene.

My girls were worried about me. They wanted me to be back to *me* again, but that was not going to happen—not yet anyhow.

I had done something a person is *not* supposed to do after the death of a spouse—I sold my house. Then I bought an old house—it eventually took six months to remodel, but it took my energies and mind away from my pain. When I finally got it finished, I moved into my wonderful new home—alone.

One evening, at the time of the day when Tim usually came home from work, my doorbell rang. It was a woman named Cindy. I had never met her, but she was to become a best friend, support system, and confidant. I will refer to her as *Cindy Two* because of another sweet Cindy in my life.

Cindy Two worked for Hospice Midland as the grief facilitator. She always reached out, especially to young widows. I answered the door with such dread, as I never wanted to face anyone at that sacred time of day. I just wanted to sit and imagine Tim walking through the door.

I answered the door anyhow, and as she came through my door, I felt a peace that I had not felt in such a long time, one that I knew was from God and that was going to get me through that next step of grief. She invited me to a support group for young widows. Oh my goodness, I had no desire to do that, nor did I want to be called the W-word, but I was kind and said that certainly I would come the next time it was scheduled.

I had already gone to another support group at FBC Midland, and to me, that was *plenty*. No one in that group really knew what grief was but me—*at least, that's what I thought*. But that is where I met my precious friend Jenny. Jenny had lost Bret the day after I lost Tim. On that first night of the support group, when I could barely speak, Jenny spoke for me, saying she totally understood my pain and would stand by my side as we walked together through this horrible time in both of our lives. Jenny and I became fast friends.

Jenny was confused; most are when they experience such deep grief, but I noticed immediately that it was something more for her. She had cared for Bret for so many years, and due to her pain from deep grief, she began having symptoms of mild cognitive impairment (MCI). Many do not realize the correlation between grief and dementia, but those two conditions often walk hand in hand. This was the case with my sweet friend, who, shortly afterward, was diagnosed with dementia and survived only five years after Bret died. She lived her last days and months in a memory-care community. Her life was devastated and ravaged by grief.

It is quite common for caregivers to have feelings of loss and grief as their lives are changed through the tireless caring of their loved ones. And Jenny had done this for Bret for over twenty years. It was a long, hard battle for her, and it showed its scars through the loss of her own health.

You will mourn him or her through this exceptionally long process—in many cases, like Jenny's—and you will experience the different stages of grief: denial, anger, bargaining, depression, and acceptance. Unfortunately, these stages do not always happen neatly or in that order. You may move in and out of different stages as time passes.

The destruction caused by your grief, however, during this process rips apart so much of who you were that sometimes the healing is impossible, as it was with Jenny.

Grief causes depression, anxiety, lack of sleep, lack of eating properly, deep withdrawal from those who could be a support for you, confusion, and memory loss. The following are symptoms shown by someone with a form of dementia: depression, anxiety, lack of sleep, lack of eating properly, deep withdrawal from those you love, confusion, and memory loss.

And we still may wonder how grief could be an onset to a dementia. Why? Because the stage of grief called *acceptance* is the hardest part—at least, it was for me.

If you're grieving, I urge you to do the following:

➢ Learn to live in the moment, a moment you never dreamed you would have to live in.
➢ Understand how the grieving process affects your life, and know that your grief is personal. Allow yourself permission to grieve in your way, with no exceptions.
➢ Appreciate the personal growth that comes from surviving loss. Be kind to yourself, and don't beat yourself up for grieving. Dig deep and find that personal growth.
➢ Find your sense of humor so you can look back on sweet memories and laugh again. Trust me, please; you will be able to do this once more.
➢ Ask for and accept help from others. Reach out and find those you can trust with your heart, knowing they love you and are willing to walk this new normal with you.

Another exceedingly difficult part of this whole dying, healing, and moving-forward process was the holidays and how to handle them. It may sound silly that I have changed lanes so quickly here, but once you walk into that first holiday alone, you will quickly realize why this is vital; it's a new aloneness like none other.

New traditions must be developed and understood by all.

Losing a loved one and walking through that first major holiday without him or her is probably one of the hardest life experiences you will have.

My first Thanksgiving without Tim was *tough*. I heard only from my brother Jim. But Jim was my stronghold throughout that first year. He never missed one day in calling me—that is 365 days that he called me, even if only for a moment, which is really all I needed. I waited for those moments, as they helped me start my day with a deep breath.

Why did no one else call me? Because no one else knew what to say. Even my mother and father didn't call me on Thanksgiving. It broke my heart. I didn't feel deserted or bitter toward them; it broke my heart because of the realization that old traditions were gone and new traditions were needed. And I was *not* ready for that.

How do you make it through those holidays—your birthday, his birthday, Valentine's Day, anniversaries, Fourth of July, family reunions (that was a big one for our family)—and then Thanksgiving and Christmas? That was when *anticipatory grief* set in. I anticipated it for days and weeks ahead of time. I tried to I follow the instructions of my friend Cindy Two and had a plan.

Just a few tips I found that worked for me:

➢ Be kind to yourself. Head to the nail salon the day before the holiday and pamper yourself.
➢ Do not feel like you must be all smiles. Grieve as only you can grieve.
➢ You are not responsible for making everyone else's day joyful. They should not expect that from you. And if they do, you are the only one who can let them know that is not part of your job description any longer.
➢ Look for moments of humor—memories that will make you smile or chuckle a little. Remember when the turkey juice overflowed in the oven at two o'clock in the morning, and the oven caught on fire?
➢ Create new traditions. Perhaps it is time for someone else to host the holidays this year.
➢ Remember that you get to make your own decisions. The only way anyone else gets the privilege of doing that is if you allow them.

Keep in mind that even though you may feel that there has never been a loss like yours, others also have faced similar losses and know what you are feeling—not exactly but similar.

Your holidays do not have to be insignificant; they can be incredibly significant in different ways. You are the one who brings that new meaning to the day, along with sharing it with those you love.

Try to grasp this thought: please don't forget that your pain is the result of much *joy and love* for the one that you lost.

Your feelings matter. You are not a robot. You have many emotions and have the right to express them. Those you love need to validate those feelings, but in the end, *you* will decide how you will weather the day.

Emotions are beneficial. Express them as only you can do for yourself. Let those who are hosting the event know that this is tough for you; that way, you'll walk in without anyone having unreasonable expectations of you.

If you need something tangible for the remembrance of your loved one during the holiday, perhaps a donation to his or her favorite charity would fill that need.

Feed your soul. Any time you experience loss, your heavenly Father can show you how to experience joy, peace, and hope once again. His love is one of the most powerful tools you can use to get through a holiday alone. He can help you find a way to carry those sweet spots in your heart of the one you loved so much.

Those we lost added such richness to our lives. Let's not let their legacy be lost due to our grief. Allow your grief to assist you in the deep sharing of their legacy.

Keep in mind that your pain represents immeasurable love—a love that can continue to be treasured, therefore easing the process of survival. It is a feeling that represents that you have been touched deeply and that you have touched someone deeply as well.

It is a time of learning that you *can* endure; you *can* be whole again; you *can* love again, without losing the one you have loved.

Chapter 8

The Process of Healing

First, there's the realization of what truly happened; then, there's the process of healing.

I'm out of denial—he is gone forever. I'm alone in my home. How do I fill that space that he once occupied?

My kids said to get a pet. I said, "My flowers are more important than a pet."

My friends said to join a good support group. I said, "Then I will be defined by my grief."

Most advice is to stay where you are, but I moved as quickly as I could; sold my home and bought another one within four months. I said, "Buy another house to flip." My kids said, "No, please." I did not listen to them. I listened to *me*.

Most advice is to make *no* major decisions, but I left my job for three months, not caring if it was waiting for me if I chose to return. I had no income, no savings, no CDs, no retirement account.

The question now is, how do I grieve the right way for me?

Let's look at my story and then at yours. Are they different? Yes, in many ways they are different. Some of the tools in your toolbox will work for you and your grief journey, but I might not have those in mine. It's sort of like when we have the flu; many medications work for flu symptoms, but I might need amoxicillin, and you might need a Z-Pak. Same illness, different ways to treat it.

We need not judge others for grieving in their own time and in their own way. We need to realize that the journey of the grief process is an especially important story that speaks volumes about who we are individually, and that needs to be told so that our healing takes place in a healthier manner for others to see.

For each of us, that is different. And those we love, who want to do everything within their power to help us through this walk, need a clear understanding of this process. My children were no exception to this rule.

They made the executive decision to clean out their daddy's side of the closet. I was in such a state that I did not care what they did; I was hanging on by a thread, and it was becoming very brittle and worn out.

About a week after Tim's death, after the girls had left, I began digging through all our stuff, and as I walked into the closet, I began searching for Tim's favorite jacket, a brown tweed. I just wanted to hold it.

It was gone. Everything was gone—his ties, his flannel shirts, his worn-out blue jeans. *But his favorite tweed jacket—surely they did not take it too. What in the world was wrong with them?*

It was a Saturday. I was in a puddle of tears, desperate to find that jacket. I grabbed a pair of sunglasses and the keys to my car and drove to Goodwill.

As I entered the store, I put my sunglasses on so no one would see the desperation in my eyes or the tears that I could not control.

I was on the hunt. I spent hours digging through every rack in the store, searching for Tim's clothes. Finally, I found the jacket, along with many flannel shirts. But the jacket was what I wanted so desperately. I gently took it off the rack, removed the hanger, and held the jacket to my face, breathing in and out to smell him. I searched his pockets; surely I would find a penny or a dime of his. But no, I found something more important: I found a toothpick.

I'd once had a horrible experience with poppy seeds in a Florida airport, while visiting with friends I had not seen in years. I laughed and talked with them, not knowing I had poppy seeds between every tooth in my head. After we said goodbye, I went to the restroom for one more potty break with my little girls before heading to the hotel and then our first entrance into Disney World.

As I washed my hands, I looked into the mirror to put on some fresh red lipstick, and to my total devastation, I saw there were black poppy seeds between each tooth, left over from the wonderful poppy seed rolls that had been a part of our lunch on the plane. I was mortified that *this* is what my friends had been staring at for over thirty minutes as we laughed and talked. From that moment forward, I never went without a toothpick in Tim's pocket to make sure I could pick out the poppy seeds after every meal.

There was the toothpick. I held his jacket close to my heart, as he was once again taking care of me, and I wept and wept.

I went to the cashier to make my purchase—here I was, buying my dead husband's jacket from Goodwill—and she said, "Oh, this is a beautiful jacket. We just got it in. Sorry that it's a little costly. It's perfect for the season we're entering, and all of our jackets are ten dollars.

I handed her a twenty-dollar bill, as I had no change. "Yes," I agreed. "It's perfect for the season I am entering also."

Then I quickly walked out of the store as fast as I could, without waiting for my change.

Grief does not come in a perfect package or on a set schedule. It comes as life's twist and turns happen.

I have met many who made suggestions as I walked this wicked path, saying things like, "This is how you will get over this quicker," or "You will never experience that feeling, and when you do, you just put it out of your mind and think of rose gardens or happy thoughts—walking with your grandchildren, playing in the sun, eating ice cream, dancing in the rain."

How insensitive they were to think they could tell me how to walk a journey that they never have walked themselves?

And imagine those thoughts—walking with grandchildren, enjoying life, as if there are no hurdles with this new walk.

I have five of the most precious grandchildren ever. I love to take walks with them. Blakely talks constantly, bringing such sweetness to any conversation. She loves to dream.

Ellis has expressions that I am certain no other child on earth has, at four years old. Everything is exciting to her, and her compassion for others, like her mother has, is indescribable.

Cannon, at five, never sits still. He is a constantly moving object, finding worms and bugs, looking for lizards, wondering what happens when the wheels of a car hit the asphalt of the road, just like his Papa Tim.

And then there is Beckett. He will be across the room from me and say, "Hey, Iddy, get ready, get set, *go*." Then he runs as fast as he can into my arms, giggling. When I leave their home, his last words to me are always, "Goodbye sugar bug." He's three.

God's love and grace gave us Briggs this past fall, so frail and tiny, yet a strong heartbeat. It was a rough road during those first few months of life, but God gave him to us to complete us, and complete we became. That sweet little boy wrapped his heart around mine and brought joy beyond measure.

Then the *wondering* of my heart begin—I wonder how to deal with the pain of knowing that my sweet grandbabies will never see the face of their amazing Papa Tim on this side of earth. He will never experience those precious moments, as I have, of playing with bugs and dolls, reading to them, coloring with them, singing with them, exploring with them as he did with our own two daughters, and seeing them come to know the Lord, as our precious Blakely did this year. The pain that engulfs me, knowing that Tim will never feel with me the joys of grandparenting is, at times, unbearable.

And then, that leaves just me; it's just me. Is that enough?

We never had an abundant income while our girls were growing up, and I always worried that we would not have a lot to provide joy and excitement for our grandkids someday, but Tim used to say, "Why, Lilly, there is no one who knows how to make chocolate chip cookies from scratch like I do. We're gonna make lots of chocolate chip cookies, walk in mud puddles, find treasures in creek beds, make tents out of quilts, and tell lots of funny stories."

I have learned that I have to make chocolate chip cookies a lot in my grandparenting world, but when those little legs come running, and arms wrap around me every time they see me, cookies seem the right way to make life happen, joyfully and with fulfillment.

I refuse to allow my "only being me" to be a barrier between me and what lies ahead of me in my relationship with my grandchildren—or, for that matter, anyone who walks into my life.

Those times of only being me were the times when I realized how *un*-alone I really was.

But finding that peace again, knowing I would be sufficient without Tim, to be an important part of life again—that was still very hard for me to grab hold of.

I found myself searching a lot.

I spent a lot of time just grasping at anything.

I went back to work rather quickly, within three weeks. I had a major conference coming up that Tim had been a major part of.

I sat in a committee planning meeting that first week after coming back to work with all of those who were a part of the upcoming event. Sitting next to me, which was the spot where Tim normally sat, was the new administrator who had taken Tim's job. She was an amazing woman; I adored her, and so had Tim. She originally had been his assistant administrator, but now she was in *his* spot.

How dare she! Why, she had no right to sit where he was meant to sit. I felt such bitterness and anger toward someone who was merely doing her job. *But it's his job! Move over!* That was what I wanted to tell her. She was such a precious friend; she was grieving also for the loss of Tim, her coworker and friend. She wanted nothing more than for Tim to be sitting in her seat.

I listened to the minutes from the last meeting, and it was as if I was hovering over the room, watching everyone speak, and I was an outside observer.

I looked over to my assistant, Alma, and said to her and the rest of the committee members, "I think you all can handle this meeting moving forward. I will see you in August." It was *May*.

As I walked out, they sat quietly, with looks of sadness and brokenheartedness for me but also total kindness and understanding. I truly was in the best place possible for support, love, and encouragement.

I went to Sue's office, the director of the Area Agency on Aging—what an amazing woman she was—and said to her, "Sue, I am leaving. I don't know when I will be back, but I will be."

She immediately got up. "Go forth. Take your time. This job and all of us will be waiting for you when you are ready." This woman was such a strong influence in my life, professionally. She had now become a stronghold in my life, personally.

I went to my office and packed the few things I thought I might need. Before I left, Terri, the executive director of the Planning Commission, walked into my office and handed me a check for $10,000. She hugged my neck and said, "We will see you when you get back. We will be here with open arms."

I drove aimlessly for several days, staying in hotels that cost over two hundred dollars a night. I found a Taco Bell, where I became a regular customer. I sat in the back, drinking sweet tea (loved their sweet tea; it was my comforter) and reading all that I could about survival as a widow. The manager became familiar with who I was and always greeted me with a smile, saying, "Got your spot waiting for you. I'll bring your tea."

I talked to anyone who would listen about my loss, my bitterness, my disbelief, and what I was going to do with it.

That was probably the most healing thing I did. Don't get me wrong; you don't want the death of your spouse to be the total focus of every conversation you have with everyone with whom you come in contact, but you also don't want that elephant in the room, where no one knows what to say and so says nothing. That only increases your feelings of loneliness.

Those stories and sharing them are part of your survival. It is comforting to share those feelings with people who understand, who love you, and who want to be a part of your healing process. More than likely, they too are grieving and need to talk about it. Your taking the lead, as you open up about your journey, brings them assurance that it won't be painful for you to let them in.

My friend Cindy Two said, "Have a plan." I trusted her totally but could not figure out how to do this *plan* thing.

She assured me there was no right or wrong way to feel. It was the process of how I dealt with those feelings that was most important.

I thought I needed to bury those feelings instead of dealing with them, realizing that was part of the process she was talking about.

I was afraid to admit I might need some medical help, a little kick to get me over the hurdle. Seeking medical attention from a trusted physician is absolutely A-OK. I had symptoms of what I thought was the flu—achiness, no energy, just *blah*. I addressed this with a doctor who knew me well, and he said, "Lilly, nothing shows me that you are experiencing the flu."

I went ballistic on him. "What kind of doctor *are* you that you can't *see* I have the flu?"

He kindly put his pad and pencil down and said, "Tell me what has recently happened in your life." He did not know that Tim had died.

That was all I needed; it was an open door to tell him about my pain. I wept, yelled, accused, and blamed the entire world for my feelings. He wept with me—did you catch that? I said he wept *with me*. He took my pain and helped carry it for me, if for just a moment.

He kindly asked if I would consider taking something medicinally to ease the edge off what I was feeling. I did not want to admit that I needed anything, but I trusted him.

You must find someone to trust to begin the process of healing.

What he prescribed was small, white, tasteless, and mighty. I took it for a year, and exactly on the date of April 21, 2008, I stopped. My need for medication was no longer there. I had learned to cope. I had found other strategies, support outlets of recovery.

Now, this does not mean that a year is a magic time frame. That means it worked for me. Remember what I have said many times—everyone grieves at their own pace and in their own time. And there is no right or wrong.

Not knowing what to expect, I continued to try to understand what I was feeling. After leaving the doctor's office, I decided I needed a long walk. I went back to that little park by the small airport, where I had boarded that medical transport plane on April 19 to journey to Dallas, to find the true answer of how we were going to make the healing process take place for my lifeless husband. Never did I realize I would once again be at that spot, looking out over the runway and finding another kind of healing process for my own heart.

Exercise was a powerful drug for me, a drug of choice that took a lot of discipline and work. But the feeling of my being important again was part of the process. I had to realize that I was needed and that my health was important, not only to me but to many others who loved me. My value was not in Tim's being a part of me; my value was in me being whole without him. I became a top priority in my life.

Eventually, however, I realized I could not go on feeling empty indefinitely, with so much anxiety and depression absorbing my entire being. I decided I was responsible for taking control of me.

At first, I did not think I needed anyone. And then, as time moved forward, I knew I needed those others who had spent much time walking this journey themselves and had much to offer me in my personal walk. I eventually realized I could not do this alone.

My goal was to shed the pain of grief and to begin to feel alive again.

No matter what other people think about your personal healing process, no one knows better than you do about what you are feeling, and no one knows better than you how to work toward your healing. You get to choose the plan that works best for you in the rebuilding process. The only ones who have the right to help you with this process are the ones you ask.

Life had to go on for me as well.

I also realized that my connections were important for the process—personal, spiritual, social, and emotional connections. They all were incredibly valuable to the healing process.

I found these through new friends. I kept my old friends, but the dynamics of those relationships changed. They had to change, as I was no longer two but one.

God brought new friends into my life, those who also had walked the same, dirty, rocky, dusty path that I was walking. That was vital. You must be patient with yourself. Realize that by connecting with others and developing new relationships, you will find that you are not alone. I decided that support groups did not define me and who I was as a person, but they gave me more clarity as to who I was—a valuable person—as one.

Worship became a vital part of my life. I continued to sit in the back row, coming in after the service had started and leaving before the last song was finished, but I did it. I went alone, as I was fearful of not being able to survive what had been a critical part of our marriage—worship. But soon, I allowed myself to absorb what God had been trying to do for me for months: show me His grace, love, and compassion for my pain. I discovered the true meaning of Romans 8:28: "And we know that all that happens to us is working for the good, if we love God and are fitting into His plan" (TLB). That is all about finding hope, joy, and peace once again.

It was on July 8, 2008, that God clearly showed me His abounding love for me. As I sat in worship, aching and searching, the pastor said, "Turn with me to Ephesians 3:16–17 in the Living Bible:"

> Out of His glorious unlimited, resources [*He has resources for me*] He will give you the mighty inner strengthening of His Holy Spirit. And I pray that Christ will be more and more at home in your hearts, living within you as you trust in Him.

So there was the key for me—trust. That is a hard one, especially if you originally blamed God for your deep loss and pain. Now, you need to trust Him.

Read carefully because this next part will be the turning point for you. When God gets our attention, He does not play games. He is real. He loved us enough to give His life for us. He knows us before we are even in the womb, so why would He want us to be in such pain?

Keep in mind that Satan is alive and well in this world also. He delights in our pain, as he wants us to believe that God is the one who caused this agony in our lives.

Satan wants nothing more than to enter certain areas of our lives so he can gain control of our deepest being. Remember that the heart is one of the strongest organs in the body. Satan's goal is to gain your heart. He will do anything he can to reach that goal. He wants to thwart the process of healing. As I have mentioned previously—but it deserves to be mentioned *very often*—Satan uses guilt to do this.

God decided that Tim would be better off dead than remaining in a marriage with me. Why? Because I was not a good wife. I did not honor him as I should have. I did not love him as I should have. I was overbearing. I did not protect us as a couple, as I should have. I was selfish. I did not appreciate him. The list goes on—I did not value the man that he was, so I am not worthy of love again. Wow, that is a heavy load to carry—and I carried it for so long.

But no more—all lies. God clearly said to me, "Let me be your protector. Do not let Satan deceive you." We must remember God's Word: "You may worship no other God, but me" (Exodus 20:3 TLB). If we are going to believe God's Word, we need to believe it all. He is our protector. He will never let us go.

A dear friend, who spent many hours allowing me to share my heart, offered me a song to lift me up. Kim Walker-Smith could not have said it better in her song, "Protector": "I come out of agreement with the lie that you have left me on my own. I am not alone. I come out of agreement with the worry and the fear I've come to know. No, they won't have a hold on me. My song in the night, Protector."

If we are going to trust, believe, and know that God is our protector, then we must let go of guilt, as it is not of him but of Satan.

Let go of Satan's grip. He holds no place in your healing process. Grab hold of the rim of God's protection.

My spouse filled more than just one role in my life. Part of the process is figuring out how to let go of his role in my life and develop ways of moving through the process of decision-making—who will take some of those roles he had? Whew, that is hard. This loss will create many empty spots in many roles that your one especially important person previously had filled.

We must come to the realization that these roles cannot be filled by that one person anymore. We need to have a willingness to reach out and allow others to come back into our lives. We need to find those people we can trust.

About a month after Tim died, I dreamed that he was sitting on the end of the bed, holding a can of Dr. Pepper. (You might remember he loved Dr. Pepper. To him, it was the answer to many struggles.)

As he sat there, he said to me, "Lilly, listen carefully, as I am going to show you the many ways this can of Dr. Pepper will assist you in daily upheavals that you encounter." Then he showed me the many ways to use that can. It was amazing. As silly as this may sound, this was Tim's way or God's way of showing me that he was my protector. I realized I could do this—through trust in Him.

I don't drink Dr. Pepper, but I have a special can, sitting on a shelf. When people ask why it's there, I tell them quickly, "It's a simple reminder of who my protector is."

Search deep for those true life preservers. We must come to the realization that guilt *cannot* play any part in our healing process; it only thwarts the process of completion.

I have given you many thoughts to process, but it is important that *you* are the one who finds the tools needed for your personal survival. It is important that *you* decide who and what will be your protector and provider to complete who you are. But keep in mind it is not those things in life that are true providers and protectors. It is the hand of the almighty God.

Chapter 9

The Promises

God's promises—what are they?

I thought it was a forever love, but now I live without that forever love. Or maybe I never knew the meaning of a forever love.

My journey without Tim was one I did not choose, nor did I ever think I would be taking it. Never in a million years would I have thought I would be forced to take this journey, yet I am taking it.

My thoughts constantly went to how long it would take me to get used to this new kind of normal.

Would I ever get used to this? Would it ever go away completely? Did I want it to go away completely? Why wasn't I given the opportunity to discuss this with Tim before he abruptly left me? So insensitive—he must not have loved me like I loved him, or he would have taken better care of himself. *Shame on him.* Forever love must not have been for *him.*

A few months after Tim's death, my counselor said to me, "Tell me what you feel."

I said, "Like an empty shell. Like I'm looking down at myself from above the ground, sort of like having an out-of-body experience. Numbness. A feeling I have never felt in my life."

"Let's take a minute to pretend you have been in a horrible train wreck," she said. "Every bone in your body has been broken, every organ crushed, bruised from head to toe. You are unrecognizable from the horrific impact of the tragic accident, yet you get up and walk away with many wounds. It is obvious you will never be the same again. There will always be scars on your body to remind you of this tragedy. You are a survivor, even though, at times, you wish you were not. There are forever aches and forever scars and forever visions of the accident. Yet you still are walking, breathing, living life."

My heart began to pound. I thought, *I couldn't have described it any better. I am the survivor of the worst train wreck ever imagined.*

For a long time, I had asked *why* and *how*. I felt such bitterness, betrayal, anger beyond measure. *Why me? I don't want to be a widow.*

Why did you have to use me as an example? Why did you have to take my husband, instead of others who deserved this tragedy? They didn't serve you, worship you, abide by your laws as *we did*. What did I do to deserve this pain? I don't deserve the agony of what a fallen world brings us. And how, God? How do I praise you in this time of sorrow? Isn't that too much to ask of a broken spirit? If you had just told me what I was doing wrong, I would have corrected it. You didn't have to go to this extreme to get my attention.

The pain was so deep, unexplainable, and something almost unrecognizable. Something that words could never describe—but a train-wrecked body came close.

I was certain that the loneliness was deeper than the deepest sea.

Confusion—how in the world would I figure this out?

Understanding—how could there ever be clear understanding for any of us?

Anger toward you, God—how could I explain to anyone the anger I felt toward you?

I decided I would not explain it; I would just hide it as best as I could.

I felt guilt over not loving Tim the way a wife should love her husband—in the simplest things, like not ironing his clothes (my opinion was that this was why permanent press was invented), cooking (those days were over), or sharing intimacy. Was that why God took him? So that he wouldn't have to suffer from being the husband of Lilly Adrian?

How dare you? I even felt angry toward Tim for leaving me.

But God, Tim was not perfect either.

I reached a point where I needed to deal with the feelings of guilt and betrayal. I asked myself, "How would Tim want me to move forward and deal with the challenges of his loss?" I knew my husband well, and he would have wanted me to do whatever necessary to deal with this new kind of normal. He'd even said so in the letter that I found. His words were, "Cling to the Father. He has this in His hands. But trust must come first."

I learned quickly that I had to acknowledge all the different levels of grief I was experiencing. I needed to guard myself from those who continued to say to me, "This too shall pass," as speedy recoveries prevent true healing; it causes great delay in the hard work that must be done. Grief recovery is *hard work*.

The world continued to turn, and mine was like a volcano about to erupt.

How would I go on? There was no manual for this part of life; at least, I didn't have one that seemed on target with what I was feeling. I had to learn how to, as my sweet mother-in-law would say, major on the majors and minor on the minors.

William Shakespeare said it well in *Richard II*: "Every substance of a grief hath twenty shadows."

And trust me, they are lurking around every corner.

I began to search feverishly for answers, reading every book I could find.

How do you put one foot in front of the other and learn to walk again? How do you learn to live when more than half of you is gone? Is it OK to cry or even yell out loud? And is it OK to just say nothing?

Silence, just being alone and in my quiet space, became a sacred time for me to just *be*.

How do you escape those feelings of emptiness, isolation, numbness, and depression? The hurt was deep within my soul.

Then, instead of asking why, I began to earnestly say, "What, God? What in the world do you want me to do with this tragedy that has been handed me?" It became noticeably clear. His Word says, "Come, I will give you rest for I give you only light burdens" (Matthew 11:38 NLT).

This was *not* a light burden to me, but I realized that God could create a blessing out of what seemed to be the greatest burden I had ever been handed. He reminded me, "That is why we never give up. Though our bodies are dying, our inner strength in the Lord is growing everyday" (2 Corinthians 4:16 TLB).

Without that inner strength He speaks of in this scripture, I could not have survived. Praise God from whom all blessings flow.

I also realized that the communication that God had so graciously allowed me to have with Tim once more—when he said in his letter, "And we will both be together again"—was a gift, a promise, a peace, given to me because God loves me and wants to be my protector from this pain.

Faith without sight is what God wants from us. He did promise to always take care of me, didn't He? He shows me something new every day.

There still are days when I feel as though I can hardly breathe, but when I see the twinkle in Blakely's eyes or the grin on Cannon's face and the sweetness of little Miss Ellis, and, of course, when Beckett runs into my arms and says, "I love you, sugar bug," and Briggs works so hard to smile at me and show me his sweet spirit, my heart becomes filled with that hope, joy, and peace I spoke about in the very beginning of my book.

There are times when I walk in the door and feel the emptiness once again, yet through it all, I know—without a shadow of a doubt—that Tim is looking down with favor on those relationships I have with our grandchildren. Oh, how I wish we could have shared them together, but I know that, someday, he too will enjoy those I have enjoyed daily and who bless me. They have taught me so much about life. For those who do not believe in a heaven with our heavenly Father, I truly do not know how they survive. I finally realized what my precious father was saying to me on April 21, 2007, when he said, "Lillian Anne, Tim is more alive today than he has ever been before. We will all see him again, and what a glorious day that will be."

The pain of letting go—really letting go—was the toughest part. I hung on for what seemed like forever to me. Then, it was like a light bulb came on, and I realized that I never had to let go, but I did have to begin to build on those precious memories by moving forward in life. Wow, Verdell Davis hit the nail on the head, during that lonely, devastating summer afternoon when she said to me, "Do you want to find joy again?" Back then, I could not imagine finding joy ever again, but I have now. It's not like I dreamed it would be, but it has hope for God's wonderful promises in my life—to take care of me and never let me go.

Do I want to love a husband again? Yes, I yearn for love in my life—that warm touch, laughter in my home, and someone with whom to snuggle, to go to church, and to eat a meal; someone to play with my grandchildren and love them deeply; someone to bring me that first cup of coffee, or better yet, someone to whom I can bring that first cup. But the question is, will I be satisfied with God's love completely? I must, as that is what true joy is.

Is that my new kind of normal, moving forward in life yet keeping those moments of joy close to my heart?

That thickness in your throat will always be there on certain occasions, and now I can thank God for that little twinge in my heart. I never thought I could say that out loud, but I have the freedom to live and know I have a story to tell. That blesses me if I know God is using it to bless someone else.

We all have stories from the heart, and we must realize that God gives us those stories for a reason. My reason became noticeably clear. It was so that when other women read this simple book, they will realize that their new kind of normal will be grieving differently than mine, but it's normal nonetheless.

Keep your eyes and heart wide open so you don't miss the blessing of the moment.

Look every day for those promises, as God has many to show you.

Chapter 10

From Why to What

Every day was a long day. I was ten months into this journey and involved in three support groups, one of which was in my own home. I kicked into servant mode. I knew my home needed to be a place of refuge for many devastated lives. I found that having folks in my house made it a home again for this grieving widow.

Many thought I was doing great, but they didn't know that I continued to try to wrap my heart around why God had to use Tim's death to bring me face-to-face with Him. This was far from my own understanding.

God, why? I need some answers, please. I just don't get it!

Why my husband?

Why did I need to be the example?

Why couldn't You have used a kinder tool to get my attention?

Why do You say in your Word, "Ask in my name, believe and ye shall receive"? I did all that, and he died. (Well, did I really do all that?)

Why take him from me when we were just beginning to share the sweetest time in our life together?

Why did You not deliver Tim from death? You could have!

Why, why, why? How could this be? Why is pain used to teach? Does God even care?

I felt deserted. I felt as though I were alone in a desert—the desert of Midland, Texas.

I felt betrayed. I felt worthless. I felt like God was no longer there.

If He is such a loving God, why did He not love me enough? But enough for what? Interesting question.

The songs of psalms were songs of praise and worship and songs of sorrow and fear. Many of the psalms were filled with those *why* questions—questions from those with broken spirits and broken hearts, experienced by all of us. Great fear, searching, heartache—that's so much a part of the grief we must walk through to find those deeply personal answers; we look hopelessly, desperately at times.

I found much comfort in seeing it in black-and-white in God's Word, so I no longer felt guilty for those whys as I searched for the whats.

Many said to me, "Your ultimate goal is to glorify God in this tragedy you are walking through." I found that almost unbelievable. Perhaps the word *appalled* better fits my reaction when I heard that statement.

I was also told, "God has a bigger plan for your life." My response was simple and straightforward: "What about *my* plans?"

> For I know the plans I have for you, declares the Lord. (Jerimiah 29:11 NIV)

Why couldn't our plans have been Your plans, Lord?
I am aching, Lord. My spirit is broken!

> For you are the God in whom I take refuge; why have you rejected me? Why do I go about mourning because of the oppression of the enemy? (Psalm 43:2 ESV)

I *beg* You to hear my cries, Lord!

> Incline your ear to me; rescue me speedily! Be a rock of refuge for me, a strong fortress to save me! (Psalm 31:2 ESV)

Face-to-face with Him—was that where He was taking me? Why didn't I see God working toward my good? You never could have told me that this would become a moment, down the road, that would work toward my good.

It was November 2017. Ten long, lonely, searching years. Verdell Davis invited me to a Women's Silent Prayer Retreat. Imagine a group of about twenty women getting together for a weekend and being *silent*. I went because I was aching. I went because I trusted Verdell when she told me that I would walk away with a new insight on silence in the Lord. I went because I was searching for answers—even ten years later.

As we began this weekend of silence, Verdell reminded us that we were there to stand before God in thanksgiving. Well, I realized quickly that I just might be in the wrong place—or was it that I was in the wrong frame of mind? Perhaps it was God's purpose for this time in my life after all.

The scriptures Verdell shared with us that first evening were all about our calling to sing praises to God.

> O come, let us sing unto the LORD: let us make a joyful noise to the rock of our salvation. Let us come before his presence with thanksgiving, and make a joyful noise unto him with psalms. (Psalm 95:1–2 KJV)

I brought a journal with me, and the very first entry I made was, "Lord, I lift your name on high."

And then my journal read something like this:

> Your perfect will for me.

> Peace, as I move forward. Always allow me to serve you! Let that be my focus.

> Who is he, Lord? I seek to see your choice for me in a spouse. I'm lonely, Lord, for this person, but I don't want to settle for less than what your desires are for me! Lord, am I worthy?

> Seeking where to serve you, Lord, in a Christian fellowship.

Note the word *worthy*.

A dear friend asked me just yesterday, "What is a word that has meaning in your life?"

At the time, I was at the car wash with my granddaughters. I asked my seven-year-old, Blakely, "If you were to choose a word that has meaning, what would it be?"

The first word out of her mouth was *worthy*.

I almost lost it. I asked her, "Why?"

She said, "Well, Iddy, we all need to feel like what we are doing is something worthwhile."

Now, this was out of a seven-year-old's mouth.

After Tim's death, I struggled so deeply to feel as though I was still worthy. I had put the value of my worth in how Tim made me feel, not in who I was in the eyes of God.

Of course, I immediately sent a text to my friend Marty, answering the question with the word *worthy*.

> Are not five sparrows sold for two pennies? And not one of them is forgotten before God. Why, even the hairs of your head are all numbered. Fear not; you are of more value than many sparrows. (Luke 12:6–7 ESV)

Wow, I am worthy, or as Blakely said, worthwhile.

We are deafened to God's voice in our lives by the busyness of the world. We have lost our sense of feeling worthy in God's sight because of the lies of the fallen world. We must remember that because of Him—and only Him—we are worthy; without Him, we are not.

We need to plan for success and favor from God. I tell those I teach, who are working with those who have dementia, that we must set them up for success at the end of each day. "Do you want to be successful?" I ask. "So do they."

We all want to be successful, but more than that, we need to be in God's favor. What does *God's favor* mean? Simple: it means worthy. We are worthy, but only because of Him.

Can I see a divine purpose in what is happening in my life?

Sitting quietly and learning to listen takes a lot of skill. Some are more natural at it, but if the truth was known, most of us are not. Now, if I can complete your sentences for you, as I so desperately wanted to do with God when it came to Tim's death, then I am a good listener. I wanted control of that situation, and I felt like God would hear my cry. He did, but His plan was bigger than mine.

Don't miss those moments of joy in the sound of a bird, a baby crying, a child laughing, a fresh spring running down a mountain side, a rainbow after a downpour.

We do not stop long enough to receive God's blessings, nor do we stop long enough to bless Him with our thanksgiving. Although it seems to be all about us, we shouldn't have guilt about those feelings, as they are very normal during this season of our lives.

But our question is, who is God in my life today?

What was His purpose for allowing this tragedy? What was His purpose for me?

Whose life are we blessing? God has blessed us with gifts. We must recognize them and use them for servanthood, not suffering. We can consume ourselves with suffering, or we can choose the path of serving. What we think is what we live out—now, that is powerful. We must develop the mind of Christ to survive this time in our lives.

We must develop the attitude of Christ to survive this time in our lives.

To live the will of God, we have to have the mind of Christ.

Quite frankly, there is no other way to live the will of God without His mindset and His attitude.

First Peter 4:10 was how my husband lived his life: "Each of you should use whatever gift you have received to serve others, as faithful stewards of God's grace in its various forms" (NIV).

Ah, His *grace.* He has given this to us as a gift. How can we serve Him? We must concentrate on servanthood, which will ease the pain of our suffering in a tremendous way.

Granted, it's not an easy path, as it's the one less traveled, and that can be scary, but it will show us more of God in every step we take. It is the only way to equip ourselves for this journey.

Do you have a regular routine to renew yourself in Christ?

We are addicted to the fear of our suffering. Read carefully to understand what I mean by *addicted.* We grab hold of it and feel no power within ourselves to be delivered from it. For some strange reason, it gives us a sense of comfort, as I shared earlier in these pages. It allows us to still *feel* the one we lost.

At this point in my journey, I can see that is so false. Only if we become addicted to God's perfect plan and will for our lives can we experience wholeness again. He is the *only* one who can deliver us from our deep pain and suffering after a loss such as this.

Please keep in mind that in our lives, we are in the fourth quarter. We must serve God and seek others who are suffering with the end in mind. That is called servanthood.

We must develop a routine for Christ. We must hunger for His Word. Now, that is a big twist, from "Why, God?" to "What, God? What do you want me to do with this tragedy in my life?"

This is where the water hits the wheel—when we can honestly say, "Lord, I come before You, seeking Your will, not mine. I come to You, Lord, not to finish Your sentences but to listen as You speak to my heart."

But, Lord—don't You despise the word *but*?

Yes, honey, you can, but

We must say to the Lord, at some point in this journey, "Lord, I hear the winds blowing. I hear the birds singing. I hear the acorns hitting the roof of my cabin, but, Lord, I want to hear You." Use that word *but* wisely!

I am ready, Lord, to let You teach me! I prepare my heart to hear You, Lord, in the silence of this moment.

I learned quickly at the Silent Retreat that I am not a very silent person. It took tons of effort for me to listen to God's Word, spoken to my heart.

It is about our willingness to be ministered to.

"I sit here, Lord, among women—kind women—who love You, Lord; women I don't even know. But I know one thing for sure, Lord—I am here because You opened the door. Lord, allow me to hear what they have to say to me, as You have brought me here to this time and place of thanksgiving, a place where I can see my worthiness because of You. Lord, is there someone here who needs me? Ah, the moment of truth! What can I do with this, Lord? How can I serve You clearly by serving others?"

One of my biggest take-aways from the Silent Retreat was that our calling is to pass on our legacy. How do I move forward and realize my legacy? I have concentrated so much on Tim's legacy that I forgot the importance of mine.

Mine is worth living for my children, my grandchildren, and, with God's blessing, perhaps even my great-grandchildren. His legacy becomes mine.

What is my legacy? They are to see faithfulness.

God can absorb all our battles:

- those of grief
- those of loneliness
- those of anger
- those of frustration and doubt
- those of not feeling worthy

I just love that word *worthy*.

Thank you, my dear friend Marty, for pushing me to think outside the box to truly realize that I am worthy in God's sight!

Lord, I think I have forgotten how to hear Your voice.

Verdell made a comment that night that has stayed with me. We all need to be able to tell someone our pain and know that person is really *listening*.

How do we really listen?

Research suggests that we only remember between 25 to 50 percent of what we hear, as shown by Edgar Dale's Cone of Experience (also known as the Learning Pyramid).

I tell my classes, "What kind of listener are you—*really*?" Many answer that they are particularly good listeners. Then I give them the test to rate their listening skills. What a revelation! There is quiet in the room as they realize that we spend more time thinking about what we want to say next than listening. Depending on our age, we may even have to jot down notes to remember what we want to say, and when the person speaking to us is finished, we have no clue what he or she has said.

We are busy taking our own notes to make sure that we know exactly what we want God to hear, while He is desperately trying to speak to our hearts.

God is not a controlling God.

God is not a forceful God.

He is a loving God who is more than willing to give us the answers to the *whats* in our lives. But because we are not at the point where we want to listen, we do not hear His voice.

He wants us to know how worthy we are to hear Him.

He wants us to know that His plan is not always on our timetable but that His plan is there and will arrive perfectly. You might remember what my very dear friend Pete said to me at the beginning of my journey, as I sat in that dark room and a doctor gave his plan—"Lilly, remember that man does not have the last word; God does." Because my head was listening, not my heart, one thing I thought he was saying to me was that my plan would be fulfilled, but as time has healed and God's Word has been revealed, I now know what he was saying to my heart: "God's plan will be fulfilled." One thing we often forget is that God wants our hearts' desires to be what His heart's desires are for our lives.

When I asked, what He clearly said to me was, "I want you to follow Me. I want you to allow Me to show you My perfect place and time for you. I want you to trust Me for this walk of a new normal."

I learned to be silent and to listen to Him speak. Oh, the words God had to share—words of comfort, peace, and deliverance from pain and sorrow; the great realization of my worthiness for His perfect love!

Chapter 11

Faith, Not Feelings

What a journey. It was a nightmare that started with a simple phone call, one that came with total disbelief, one I will never forget. It's such a story of devastation, anguish, grief beyond measure—and pure joy and promises of God's never-ending love. This journey is not over and won't be until death.

Yes, the pain is still there. Regardless of what people say—people who haven't experienced grief as I and perhaps you have—the pain does *not* go away, but it's a pain now of daily growth in God's Word. If we don't claim His Word, we can never put one foot in front of the other.

When I first read the scripture that says, "Count it all joy, my brothers, when you meet trials of various kinds" (James 1:2 NLT), I thought, *What a harsh God He is.* But now I see clearly—not every day, but for today, I understand. It's that childlike faith that brings us to our knees. It's the realization that He can *and will* bring us out of our sorrow, and we will bring praise to Him from our lips.

God has taught me much through many people. I have made many mistakes, but I have learned through those mistakes. One thing I learned quickly is that we are mere seed planters in the lives of those God brings our way. I want them to know my Lord in the way I know Him. I can only hope that those with whom I share the Lord with will someday see Him as their means of hope and eternal life. That is where the seed planting comes in and faith the size of a mustard seed—that God is almighty, and He alone can nurture that seed.

I had a great teacher for eleven years, after moving to Dallas from Midland. His name was Dave Fortune; he left this world a few months ago after much physical suffering, but I need to tell you what this man taught me. He taught me to *never* miss an opportunity to share the gospel. He taught me that it needs to be free-flowing, as we speak to anyone, that Jesus Christ is Lord. We are His witnesses; it is His command to us, and if we do not use life's tragedies for His glory, we have failed Him.

As I sat in Dave's memorial service, a time of true praise and worship, I watched his sweet widow, Jean, smile with the honor of being blessed with him as her husband for over fifty years. I thought, *I understand the pain she is experiencing 100 percent, but the strength she has in the Lord took me years to grasp.*

Jean was the inspiration that got me back on my computer to complete this book. She showed me, as did her sweet husband, that life *does* bring joy; that there is such importance for us to continue the legacy of those who have gone before us, and we must not let those great legacies die.

Dave is more alive today than ever before. Why? Because he trusted the Lord and shared that trust, as we should do daily. Many seeds will continue to burst wide open due to his servant's heart. Death does not seal us in a grave; we continue to live, for years to come, through our sharing of Christ's love. That is the reason why Tim Adrian's faith in the Lord has not died but is still being shared through those with whom he shared so passionately.

This gave me a reason to live, to rejoice, and to praise God during my time of brokenness.

One of the gifts that Jean gave to each of us in attendance at Dave's Celebration of Life service was a list of the many scriptures he had written down in some of his study notes, which I will cherish forever. One of those scriptures spoke to my heart with much richness and peace:

> The Lord is my rock, my fortress, and my deliverer. (Psalm 18:2 NIV)

If you are where I was, I can tell you that many people will walk into your life during your time of finding that new kind of normal, and God will use them to bring you through this terrible journey. But it will not be without the strength of your heavenly Father. He alone is the only one who desires your total trust and faith in knowing that He will never let you down. As His Word says, He will be your rock, fortress, and deliverer. We must continue to walk in His light, looking for His promises, because we must lean on that which is steadfast and true.

I miss being *two*. I miss sitting in restaurants with someone with whom I can share a meal. I miss having someone with whom to worship. I miss having someone to do my returns for me, someone to fix leaky pipes, someone to grill chicken and burgers. I miss having someone to join me in playing with my grandchildren, someone who brings me that first cup of coffee of the day, someone to take Saturday side trips with me. I miss having someone to help me plant flowers or mow the grass, someone for whom I can cook new recipes, someone to drive in my black Ford Thunderbird, someone who knows my life stories, and someone who is presently a witness to my life and who loves the Lord Almighty.

I miss all of that—and tons more.

Love as we once experienced—like we sometimes see in the movies or when we were fresh out of college—is not what we search for in new relationships after loss. Our desires are for relationships to come back to us in totally different packages. There is so much more that we need and want after a loss. Love looks more like companionship, friendship, someone to connect with us who understands our journey and, oh yes, that sweet lover of the heart intimacy that only God can ordain and bless; someone who will allow us to continue to love the person that we lost yet allow us to move in a different direction as we build new memories for a continued lifetime with someone new. It's someone to love us with all those broken pieces and who is willing to help us put those broken pieces back together again.

This new relationship should become one of the healthiest relationships you have ever experienced. This *someone* will see you like no one else has ever seen you. And he or she will allow you to grieve exactly in the way you need to grieve for as long as you need to grieve.

The most important thing that you, as the one experiencing such a loss, needs to grab hold of is that *you will be happy again*. Oh, there will be tremendous moments of grief forever and times when you will ache from the absence of your spouse, but you can and will have a full and meaningful life once again. You will realize that your thoughts fall back on sweet memories and precious joy that creates a foundation for life to be complete again.

Our time of grief and the way we grieve may become almost sacred to us. We grieve not only for our loss but for those who also have lost this loved one; we grieve over what we can never get back. We search high and low for ways to get beyond it, to escape some of the pain before us. As you walk through this grief, know that there is no way around it, under it, or over it; you must go *through* it. Do whatever it takes to gain the support you need from family, friends, support groups, and, above all, from your heavenly Father. He is steadfast and will never let you down.

He grieves with you.

His Word is clear on our future for those who love Him and honor Him.

> He will wipe away all tears from their eyes, and there shall
> be no more death, nor sorrow, nor crying, nor pain. All of
> that will be gone forever. (Revelation 21:4 KJV)

Look for His promises and rely on them to walk you through this journey of loss. With God, there is completeness once again, if only we will trust. He can protect us from those tragedies on our pathway of life. Again, we must hold on to the fact that His desire for us is to walk by faith not by sight. Many times, we don't understand His provisions for us. In my loss, my protection came in the form of peace and strength in the middle of despair. It's hard to recognize that God's protection sometimes comes as an *ending* to a devastation in life that He knows we cannot hurdle alone, nor can we see over the horizon of what He already knows.

He wants us to come to Him as His child, as we would come to our earthly fathers, asking Him to allow us to be cradled in the arms of His love and protection. He wants to hear us say, "I cannot live without You, Father. I cannot face tomorrow without You, Father. Today I choose for You to carry me, as I so desperately need You to do. I come to You with a childlike heart, hungry to feel Your tender care."

Life has many moments of changes, those we want and those that we prayed we would never have. Many of those changes, like the death of a spouse, will leave us motionless at times. But I can promise you that through the dust and ashes of the loss, you will find new, rich soil. And as we plant our feet on God's Word, we will see His grace and love peeking through the hopelessness. If we water that grace and love with rich prayer and communication with God, He will teach us to run, not walk once again.

Life will never again seem the same—how could it when he or she is gone? When we finally get that and are OK with getting it, then we are able to move forward. We have removed ourselves from the fix-it mode.

Let me share a smile with you with the tale of the two turtles.

My precious little Ellis and her sister Blakely had two turtles, Gretta and Piggy. Those two little girls loved those little turtles deeply. The girls opened a lemonade stand one day and put Gretta and Piggy in a little crate next to them, to keep them safe while they were busy selling cold lemonade.

Turtles are quick, however, and after they were left without supervision for only a few minutes, they pushed the crate door open and entered the world of the free. When the girls realized this, the stages of grief took place. At first, they were in denial—"Oh, they are around here somewhere." Then they panicked; surely the turtles could not be gone forever! "Oh no, we are never going to find them! They are *gone!*" That was acceptance; then the grieving began.

Blakely was devastated and wanted to know *how* this possibly could have happened. Then came the *why* and then the *what*—what should she have done differently? She was concerned that she might be responsible for the cause, as she and Ellis continued to hunt up and down the alley, in corners of the yard, under bushes. This just could not be true! After much searching for answers to *why*, Mom and Dad did all they could to reassure the girls that those sweet turtles were at a better place, probably swimming in someone's pool on such a hot day.

Blakely ached for hours and even into the next morning. She woke early to begin her search again, as she knew she would find them and this nightmare would be over.

My daughter Kelly, the girls' mother, was busy the next morning, getting things ready for their day, Ellis walked in and quietly said to her mom, "Mommy, I'm not really so sad about losing Gretta and Piggy. Is that OK that I'm not as sad as Blakely is?"

Grief comes in different packages. And why do we need to ask permission to grieve our way? Human nature says we do, but read this carefully: *we don't.*

If we don't attend to grief, it sometimes will rear its ugly head when we least expect it, so not attending to it properly may thwart the healing process and make it much more difficult down the road. Recognizing our grief makes our healing process healthier. Denying it makes it darker than the darkest night you have ever witnessed.

The realization that life can be lived again is part of trusting God, our Father, who is more than able and willing and wants to bring us through the rough territory called grief. None of us is worthy, except through the Lord, Jesus Christ. Praise God, He is such a forgiving God because this sinner, saved by grace, needs forgiveness daily.

God has always been there—He never turned away from me—with His love and grace. When you know Him better and feel Him every day as He walks with you, you realize that you *are* worthy in His eyes. My spirit hungered and thirsted to be closer to Him, as He was my comforter, my protector, my everything. I was able to journey through this train wreck of a tragedy because God picked up the pieces, put me back together, and showed me that He would never leave my side. That is why I walk today with joy, peace, and hope for all He has done for me.

There are times when I feel that I am not seen or heard. My life has not gone as I planned, and I still search daily for how to get back to where I was. It was painful when I realized I will not ever be back to where I was. Yet it is during this time of greatest loneliness that God can reveal His presence to us.

His Word is oh-so-comforting to me. I am certain this was part of God's plan throughout this tragedy—to bring me to a point of hunger for His Word. He wanted that intimate relationship with me. He is lonely for us. Imagine not hearing from your children for months while they are away at college. Mine never seemed to call home unless they needed something—at least, they didn't call enough to suit me.

We do not call enough for God either. Yet He is so faithful and brings us through those valleys to teach us about His great love for us, to teach us to depend on Him. We will find ways of strength and endurance through Him so we can push through the grief as He guides us with His Word.

The Bible tells us that the pain of losing a spouse is both cruel and long-lasting. "When Sarah passed away, Abraham, her husband, came and mourned Sarah and wept over her" (Gen. 23:1–2 KJV).

Despite having great faith in the Lord, Abraham felt intense grief when his precious Sarah was gone.

Some have said there is nothing more stressful, nothing that causes greater pain, than losing a spouse. You have a feeling of emptiness, a feeling that one has with the disability of not being able to walk—a crippling feeling.

As those who support the one who lost a loved one, we should never view their tears, confusion, or deep sadness as a weakness; instead, we should show empathy and support for as long as they need us.

Remember that there is no right or wrong way to grieve, nor is there a time frame of grief or a plan to follow. We must allow ourselves to grieve in the best way we can for *us*, not allowing anyone to impose their answers to our grief timelines.

Matthew 6: 34 brought me great strength: "Don't be anxious about tomorrow. God will take care of your tomorrows. Live one day at a time" (TLB).

To many, these words of our Lord apply to material needs in life, but for me personally, they have helped me to walk through this journey of the loss of Tim. He was my provider, breadwinner, emotional support, and the spiritual leader in our home. So I write this to bring peace about God's care for you. He has your back. He will be your provider.

In my case, thirteen years later, He has never failed me.

You too can have that same joy, peace, and hope as you walk this journey, even though it seems unbearable at times. You might not believe that now—you might not even want to hear it—but give yourself some time, and then come back to these pages, and you will see the words so clearly.

The world assumes that grief should last for a short time; if it doesn't, you are considered weak, as moving forward quickly shows strength. What a falsehood that is. True strength is shown by in whom we put our trust. A heartbreaking trauma has the power to change our lives forever; in fact, it does. But in whom we put our trust has more power than the trauma itself—despite how hard that is to believe in moments of deepest sorrow— to bring healing to our broken hearts. It is the way we turn our faces that matters. Do we turn away from hope into a life filled with bitterness and hopelessness, or do we turn our faces toward the light, the Son, that light hope and faith that only God can bring about? Sometimes, that's all we can hold on to.

When we can no longer see, we must remember it is not by sight but by faith that we must walk to see the light at the end of the journey. We must believe in God's timing and realize that it's not always ours, and it may not be an answer we can comprehend. Accepting where we are seems nearly impossible. We may feel undeserving of such pain, but what makes us exempt from this pain, versus the next guy? We must humble ourselves, on our knees before the Lord, to clearly see and understand where He is taking us.

I am still not always clear. I am still lonely many times. I find myself on one knee, instead of two. Trust in God is not a magic pill. It does not make the pain go away as if it never happened. You might remember that I said to Verdell Davis that I never wanted to let go of the pain from the loss of Tim because that pain represented him. If I let it go, I was letting go of the last of him here on earth. Think about that for a minute. Our trust cannot be seen from a long-term interest but from a short-term, day-by-day walk.

Accepting our tragedy and surrendering those scars and pain to our heavenly Father is truly the only way we can survive; that's how I see the battleground. And friends, trust me; it is a battle and a hard one. We must know that the greater plan is something that's not possible without the faith needed to know that the Lord is carrying us. We need to commit to His greater power to walk through this new journey, seeking His face as we search for a new hope. And it is a day-by-day decision to do this.

God's Word says that we must trust in Him and pour out our hearts before Him, for He truly is our only refuge.

Many times, I felt as though I had been cheated. I thought that I was doing what God wanted me to do with my life, alongside my husband. I worked hard, serving and pleasing God in all my daily works. But He does not judge us by our works. I knew that in my head-knowledge, but my heart-knowledge told me something else, that my journey of serving God was over because I no longer was complete. I felt like I had lost my drive and that all my hard work had been done in vain.

Then God's Word once again became clear to me. I remembered Paul encouraging the Christians in Philippi with the following confident words—he had no doubt that God would finish the good work He had begun in their lives:

> And I am sure of this, that he who began a good work in you will bring it to completion at the day of Jesus Christ. (Philippians 1:6 ESV)

That all sounds good, but how does God do that when we are so empty and alone? Four simple words: we abide in Him.

> Abide in me, and I in you. As the branch cannot bear fruit by itself, unless it abides in the vine, neither can you, unless you abide in me. I am the vine; you are the branches. Whoever abides in me and I in him, he it is that bears much fruit, for apart from me you can do nothing. (John 15:4–5 ESV)

We must learn to listen for His voice again in our lives, as we often become dormant in that relationship during those deepest, darkest hours. Survival cannot happen without that key element—abiding in Him; staying close to Him.

He knew about that call before I did. He knew before I knew about that loss. He knew before I knew about my many scars and brokenness, and He knew He would bring me to completion once again. What a sigh of relief that brings to my heart. It's not up to me; He's got this!

Completion today will not look like completion yesterday. Your circumstances may have changed but God has not. As your heart mends, you will find those moments of strength, and you will wonder, *How did I do this?* You might even feel some guilt because you did not need your spouse to complete a task that was once his. Looking back, you will see the spot you were in and realize how uncomfortable it was. You will realize the need to move in a direction of fulfillment. You will slow your pace down just long enough to see the wonder of his world around you, and you will find that *ahhh* moment of complete rest.

Do you remember the fairy tale *Little Red Riding Hood*? She went to her place of joy, her grandmother's house, but she was not aware that there was wickedness in the forest. That wicked old wolf could not have cared less about her; He only wanted to make her stumble so she couldn't find joy safely. As she walked along the path to Grandmother's, she left her trust to the unknown; she relied on her instincts that she was on the right path and would safely get to Grandmother's house and home again.

You know the rest of the story—much turmoil and fear walked into her path, but ahead of her was the home she sought. Protection and love; fear is gone; faith without sight as a little child.

God has created a safe path for us to follow. This moment of realization is pivotal in our healing process.

> You are of God, little children because He who is in you
> is greater than he who is in the world. (1 John 4:4 NKJV)

All that you were and all that you are is a sacred place to which God has so gently taken you. He can, if you just allow Him, begin the healing of those broken pieces and scars that left you feeling tossed into a world of disbelief. He can restore you to a vessel of hope, joy, and peace, as He can for many who are just beginning this journey of finding a new kind of normal.

I need you to know: God is the *only* reason I am where I am today.

> For He will hide me in His shelter in the day of trouble;
> He will conceal me under the cover of His tent; He will
> lift me high upon a rock. (Psalm 27:5 KJV)

He is the rock of my salvation!

As we were going through Tim's computer after his death, we received a gift from him, one that I would call a little wink from God.

Please read the following story, written by Tim, to bring you hope for tomorrow. We must realize that *today is tomorrow's yesterday.*

Chapter 12

Today Is Tomorrow's Yesterday

Penned by Tim Adrian, date unknown

It is kind of a funny feeling, when you get to an age, and you suddenly realize that you are eighty years old! Today is that day, and I have been looking forward to it for the last eight decades. It seems like only yesterday that Lilly and I were getting married; that was over fifty-five years ago. My how time flies. I grew up thinking that eighty years old was old! But now, it kinda feels like turning forty again; you know something is *supposed* to be different in your life, but you do not *feel* any different. I can still play golf, work around the house, and play with the grandkids and the great-grandkids. (Now that does sound kind of old, doesn't it?)

Last week, when I was at the Y swimming laps, I noticed that group of young ladies in their forties doing their water exercises, and I thought to myself, that exercise must be good for you, 'cause I've been doing it for the last fifty years, and I'm still going strong. Not as quick, not as far, not as fast, but still going. Isn't that what life really is all about? A little arthritis, a low-back ache when I work too hard or bend over the wrong way. My eyes don't see as good as they used to, and the macular degeneration is getting a little worse, but I can still see to hit a golf ball, read my Bible or a newspaper, and play with the grandkids!

"Lilly, I'm going down to the RV building to drink coffee with the old men! I'll be back around 8:00." You know, I've checked in with her for over fifty years. She is doing better, now that the doctor has her heart rhythm and blood pressure where it ought to be. She still looks pretty good for a seventy-nine-year-old bride, and well, never mind.

I really enjoy living here in this retirement neighborhood. I have always enjoyed old folks, and now I am one! The walk from our garden home to the RV is about two blocks and is a good time to just think about life and where it has gone and where it is going. This campus finally filled up. I thought we would never be able to find the right way to make this place work!

"Hey, you old coots, what are you old men doing out of the house without an ambulance nearby?"

I walked into the RV and met my group of guys who I drink coffee with every day, solve the world's problems, and sometimes really get to share some of the burdens of living. Good group of guys, from widowers to a couple who are not well for their age at all, and then there's Ben, who cares for his wife with Alzheimer's. He really should not leave her alone, but he says she is safe for an hour since she is sleeping. But he really looks tired a lot.

"Old coots? Who are *you* calling old? You are the one who cannot shoot his age anymore! Hey, bald man, sit down before you fall down, and don't drool when you drink your coffee this time!" That is Ben, always willing to start the day off right!

"Good morning to you too, Ben; glad to see you haven't lost your manners. Looks like we are all here this morning. No one died last night; that's a good start for the day!" We all laughed and hooted with each other. It is fun to have them pick on you. It is about the only way the guys will tell each other that they love each other, by picking on each other. But I know they care, and they know I care.

"Hey, Paul, are you going on that senior adult church trip to Missouri with us?" Paul lost his wife about a year ago and really has not gotten over it. We cannot get him to do much of anything.

"I don't know. I'll let you know." That is just his way of saying no.

I noticed that the guys were unusually spunky this morning. Paul reached under the table and brought out a small package, wrapped like it had been wrapped by a third-grader, but wrapped. Then he said, "Happy birthday, you old man! Welcome to the world of the eighties!" They sang, croaked, and squealed "Happy Birthday" to me and told me to open the package.

As I *slowly* unwrapped the package, just to make them squirm, I could not imagine what they had gotten, probably a box of ex-lax or something like that. The white box was light and looked sort of like a handkerchief box. I opened it up, and there was a brown-cotton work glove inside. But something was different about this glove; the fingers were cut off; it had no fingers!

"Oh, what a surprise, and just my size. How did you know?" We all laughed.

"Try it on!" they said.

"OK," I said. So I pulled the soft brown glove out of the box and slipped it on to my right hand. It fit funny since it had no fingers or thumb. "OK, what's the deal with the no fingers? What did y'all do? Find it at a garage sale?" I was looking at how funny my hand looked with just the fingers pointing out so I didn't notice that each of the guys had their right hands on the table, and then I noticed that each one of them had one of the fingers from the glove on their fingers. Dave had the thumb, Paul had the index, Ben had the middle finger, Steve had the ring finger, and Robert had the pinkie.

Ben spoke up and said, "Tim, just like that glove isn't complete without the fingers, we aren't complete without you. And if ever you need help with anything, just remember there are five of us willing to give you a hand. I guess you could say we are hand-in-glove kind of friends. Thanks for your life. Happy birthday, you bald-headed old coot!"

It all hit me then. The dreams, the prayers, the work, the laughter, the tears of frustration and joy—yesterday's toil becomes today's treasure, and tomorrow never really gets here. These guys had just made my life worth living eighty years! What a group of loving men. "Yesterday I was thinking about tomorrow, which is now today. I really was not looking forward to this birthday. Eighty is just too close to being old. But you know what? I would not trade today for any of the best days I have ever had in the last eighty years—well, except for my wedding night! You guys are great. I love all of you!" We all laughed, shook hands, and hugged. Now, that is living.

If you ask me to look back and see why I am the way I am now, I will encourage you to keep looking at today. Because today is the tomorrow of yesterday. I live every day to the fullest. When I pray, I talk to a loving God who loves me and the way He made me. When I play with kids, I try to get them to enjoy the dandelions and clouds of today because tomorrow, they may not be here to enjoy. There was a time in my life when these sorts of things were foolish to me. But I remember losing my grandfather nearly fifty years ago, like it was just yesterday. He and I both were cut-ups. He worked hard all his life to live in a frame house at the end of a dusty road, not in the best part of town. But he *was* the best part of town. He was a milkman, a water-meter reader, and finally a nursing home janitor. He laughed at life; no, he laughed with life. A man whose word was better than a contract. He enjoyed fresh pears off his tree and would hold us up so we could pick one to eat. He taught me that work was a way of being who you really are. He always said, "If you are a grump at home, then you will be one at work too." How true, how true. I cherish the beauty of today. He taught me that. I taught my kids that; they taught their kids that. Yesterday, one man influenced my life. Now, over fourteen lives, just in my family, have been influenced for the better. He did not quote the Bible much, but he lived it out a lot.

Oh, I get in the dumps some. But all I have to do is look around and either enjoy where I am today or see someone, like Ben, who would trade anything in the world if he could get his dear Mary healed. God has promised to never give us more than we can handle. Hang in there, Ben.

"I'm home, hon," I said as I walked into the house.

"So did you solve the world's problems today?" Lilly looked at me and said, "Happy birthday, birthday boy!" We kissed, and then she noticed the glove on my hand. "What is that?" she said, giggling.

I said, "Do you remember that first patchwork quilt that I got you when the kids were young? You know, the one with the flannel backing? Remember the note that the girls and I wrote about the quilt and how much you meant to us?"

Lilly looked at me kind of funny and said, "Why, of course I remember; how could I forget? I still have that note in the cedar chest."

"Well, this is my quilt from the guys, and each one of them has a finger. Who would have thought yesterday that tomorrow would have turned out so good today!"

Today is Tomorrow's Yesterday. Penned, by Tim Adrian

Chapter 13

His Awesomeness Revealed

When we experience tragedy in our lives, how can we, as human beings, truly say, without a doubt, "I can praise God"?

What are those moments that bring us to this point?

Even after knowing God personally for most of my life and experiencing His goodness so many times—through the eyes of my children and grandchildren, through the freshness of the rain, through the laughter of friends and family gathered together, through the warmth of a simple fireplace, and the joy of achievements that only He could have made possible—it still becomes a challenge to see His goodness in the midst of pain.

It comes down to a simple act of trust, realizing that He is all-knowing; He has walked before us, behind us, and with us.

I know that throughout this pain, He has His perfect plan for us in His hands, and we have much joy to look forward to, in spite of the pain.

Sometimes, it is searching hard for those little moments, as I did so often.

I remember the first wedding anniversary without Tim, only thirty days after his death. May 21, 2007. I waited for the clock to strike midnight on May 20. I grabbed my car keys and headed out into the darkness of the night with no fear. I headed to the nearest grocery store that was open twenty-four hours a day. There, I went to the card aisle, one I had frequented many times since living in Midland for those last-minute special-occasion cards. I was panicked, knowing I had not—for the first time in thirty years—gotten my sweetheart an anniversary card. I must, as if I did not, then his death was more of a reality, and that was not what I wanted. I wanted to wake up from this nightmare, and denial was the best route for me to take. As I opened many cards and read the sentiments; nothing quite fit what I wanted to say. Then, there was a card filled with joy, sweet memories, and thankfulness for who he was in my life. That is what I wanted to say. With tears streaming down my face, I bought my card and went home. Once inside those doors, I found my safe spot where I could cry, be angry, ask questions, and weep without shame, knowing that God understood my pain.

For that moment, I needed to know that Tim loved me, throughout all of our marriage, as deeply as I loved him, that he chose me for all the right reasons. I needed affirmation that my marriage had been blessed by God, that it was not just a past moment but always would be one of those blessed gifts with which God had honored me. Once again, I asked God to allow me that feeling of assurance.

I pulled the covers up over my body and settled in for the night, knowing my next day would be spent on the road to Abilene to carry that card to the grave and spend time with the love of my life. Even thought my head-knowledge knew his spirit was not in that grave, not the man he truly was, my heart-knowledge was aching, as I knew that is where his body lay.

As I woke the next morning, I began searching through his old army trunk, where he stored all his stuff from years gone by. There were high school band medals, Boy Scout patches, vacation Bible school certificates, and a few prayer journals from when he was attending Baylor University, where he came to know the Lord. And then there was a legal pad, very old, yellowed, with many notes written in pencil. The very first page was budget notes, written for our first month of marriage. Then, there was a page on tasks that he needed to complete for our wedding date, May 21, 1977. Then there was the third page, titled "Reasons Why I Should Marry Lilly." I sat in astonishment of God's awesomeness becoming more real to me in that very moment. I had asked, and God had honored my request for affirmation of Tim's love for me.

It went something like this:

1. Because she is a woman of integrity
2. Because God brought her to me

3. Because she loves the Lord
4. Because she loves me
5. Because I love her more than life itself
6. And why not. Because she is beautiful!

I smiled, cried, laughed, and felt God's presence—and Tim's presence—in that very moment. I thanked the Lord for one of the greatest gifts ever. I clearly heard Him say to me, in my spirt, *I am with you always. Tim's love will always be with you also.*

Much healing began that very moment. Yes, much pain still followed through those many months after Tim's death. But God's allowing me to see His very presence in my life at that moment brought me to the realization of His undying love for me and that He was on this journey with me and would never let me go. I learned the importance of speaking His truths—those biblical truths—over my pain.

It is imperative that we believe God's biblical truths and that He loves us, never allowing anything to affect that unconditional love, and that He *does* have a perfect plan for us to unveil in His time. There will be times of unrest, struggles, and pain so deep that we feel as though we cannot catch our breath, but through it all, we will have much clarity that God will carry us through this turbulent time in our lives.

Did I want to walk this journey? Absolutely not. Did I believe that God held me gently in His strong arms throughout this storm of life? Absolutely yes. Did I feel God's love wrapped around me at all times? No, not really. But head-knowledge and heart-knowledge are very different, and God protects us through both.

It was at the feet of Jesus when I lay across the floor of my living room and cried out to Him to wrap Himself around me, and I gained peace. It was during those most vulnerable times that He would say to me, "The Lord himself goes before you and will be with you. He will never leave you nor forsake you" (Deuteronomy 31:8 KJV).

I have mentioned many times that I searched high and low for rainbows; that this was one of the ways God showed me His many promises of His love and His assurance that He was walking this journey with me. There were times when I begged Him for rain to wash away my pain. And then

I realized it was through those rainstorms that He alone brought me strength.

Satan would love to know that he still has control over our pain. But God is our fortress and our protector, and that can never be taken away from us.

I moved to Dallas twelve years ago to be closer to my children. I immediately began searching for a church home and a fellowship of believers who would give me support and encouragement at a very dark time in my life. During that search, I found a fellowship like none other. It is called Friends for the Journey and was exactly what I needed.

Many changes have taken place over these last few years within this group of believers, and the faces of this group look very different than when I walked into this group for the first time. But one thing that has never changed is the love of the Lord that they each have. Their faith through all walks of life never fails them. They struggle, but they come together and support and encourage each other. I hear Andre's prayers for his brother, mother, and neighbors, and I listen to Bill speak with joy about his grandchildren and the love he has for his children as he prays for them fervently. I see the journey that Kurt walks each day in faith, believing God's protection over him. I listen to Clayton read God's Word and share his thoughts with us on our need for God's love and God's need for our commitment to His Word. I listen to Margaret's many words of great wisdom and faith throughout her life's journey and her sweet compassion for people within our community. She speaks of her precious daughter, Kim's, love for life itself and those sweet children she ministers to each and every day because of God's love. Then I hear Steve bring to us God's Word, the history of His Word, and his unfailing love for us, and I walk away with more knowledge than ever of God's awesome promises and protection for His children.

We all must have friends for this journey called life. It is impossible to walk without those people who walk with us, those people who too know the awesomeness of our Lord.

Please seek that fellowship. There is no way to journey this new kind of normal without the support of friends who will become your encouragers while praying for you. They will become witnesses to your life.

"Father God, thank You for Your constant reminder of how much You love me. I will forever be grateful for the daily strength You bless me with to walk the journey of life itself. Allow me to become more aware daily of the need for me to share this love with others who are walking a journey of pain and sorrow. Allow me to be a friend for the journey of those who cross my path, in need of Your love, as this is your command for each of us who loves You and are called to serve You.

It is in Your precious Son's name that I pray and praise You.

Amen."

Chapter 14

What Is Your Story?

Writing your story in black and white so you can see it, read it, read it again, and then take time to share it will speed the healing process. So here is the challenge: begin writing. Nothing is right or wrong, as this is yours, only for your eyes to see and your heart to ponder, until you are ready to share it, if that time even comes. This is for you.

Let me try to frame it for you with some thoughts or questions to get you thinking. If you don't need to ask these questions, then what are your own questions? The following questions are many I asked myself as I journeyed through my walk. As I took each day, one step at a time, I needed reassurance that I was walking in accordance to God. Also, I've shared some of the scriptures that allowed me to see how God's Word has been so faithful throughout my journey.

* Who am I now, Lord?
    For the Eyes of Lord are on the Righteous and His Ears are attentive to their prayers. (1 Peter 3:12 NLT)

* How do I learn to walk again, breathe again, and exist as one?
    The Lord is near to the brokenhearted and saves the crushed in spirit. (Psalm 34:18 NIV)

* How do I gain the desire to live life to its fullest again?
  And to know this love that surpasses knowledge that you
  may be filled to the measure of all the fullness of God.
  (Ephesians 3:19 NLT)

* It's a couples' world, God, and I'm lonely.
  For He has said, I will never leave you nor forsake you.
  (Hebrews 13:5 ESV)

* How do I find those promises, Lord, that You are my protector?
  Peace I leave with you. My peace I give to you do not let your
  heart be troubled and do not be afraid. (John 14:27 NLT)

* How do I find joy, peace, and hope in You, Lord?
  Consider it great joy, my brothers and sisters, whenever
  you face trails of many kinds, for you know the testing
  of your faith produces perseverance. (James 1:2–3 NLT)

* Lord, I am afraid of this new normal. How do I walk it alone and
  without fear?
  You are my hiding place; you will protect me from
  trouble and surround me with songs of deliverance.
  (Psalm 32:7 NIV)

Finding God's words of truth, wisdom, and encouragement were necessary for me to move forward and realize His purpose for me. I don't think I ever saw His Word come to life until this tragedy. Being a Baptist preacher's kid kept me in the church, but not in the Word. It's God's Word that brings us life rich with peace that surpasses all understanding.

We are told in 1 Corinthians 13:12 that we only know part of what God wants to show us with His loving promise that we, as His children, will one day know all the joy He has prepared for us. This says to us that God did not create the tragedies of life; instead, He allowed the possibility for sin to enter our lives. We have free will as humans to accept these moments of crisis as part of His will to bring us growth and the realization of His mighty power. That does not mean we will always have a clear understanding of these moments, but we can know that God grieves with us and wants to carry our pain, if we will simply trust Him.

Our choices of how we walk this journey is what truly matters. Our not understanding it in its totality does not mean God's promises to us are not real. It means we are at a turning point of trust and blind faith, knowing He is there to hold us up, to never let us fall without His precious grace protecting us.

Remember the word Paraclete that I mentioned in the beginnings of this book? He cries out to us to be that Paraclete. The words *blind faith* become clear. Walking by His light, not ours. Knowing He is the protector, the deliverer of pain and emptiness.

He is the only one to once again bring us into the fullness of life.

As Verdell said to me so many times, do you want to find joy again? This only comes by trusting God blindly, knowing He will never leave us without His loving Spirit wrapped around us.

So again, I ask you: what is your story? Trust me when I say that it is *not* a story He has not heard yet. He will handle your story as if it's the only story that's important at this very moment, if you will just allow Him to love you through each step. He wants you to find His purpose for you again.

> You are my hiding place; you will protect me from trouble
> and surround me with songs of deliverance.

—Psalm 32:7 (TLB)

Chapter 15

Living with Purpose Again

God so sweetly wants us to come to the "end of ourselves," as Rebecca St. James sings in her song "Dawn," and to allow Him to "water the garden of our lives with the many tears we have shed. He is so faithful."

How faithful are we in trusting Him?

He is there, patiently waiting for you to investigate His face for the answers to your questions. He is there, wanting to hear you call out His name. He is there, eagerly waiting to see that the desires of your heart will be in His perfect plan for your life, that plan that He had chosen for you since birth.

Can you wrap yourself around this thought? Tim was a gift to me. I did not own it; he was gifted to me but for a season in my life.

Purpose: intentionally live for God.

> Whatever you do, work at it with all your heart, as working
> for the Lord, not for men. (Colossians 3:23 NIV)

How do we live intentionally?

First, we must recognize God's deep desire for us to live in His plan and intentionally work toward that goal.

Second, we must thank Him for our purpose and for the many gifts He has given us and that we recognize are gifts only for today. We must ask Him to show us the ways He desires for us to use the gifts He has given us.

Third, we must choose to live intentionally for Him. There is that word again—*choice*. We must choose to use the many blessings and gifts He has given to us to glorify Him. Once we know our purpose, through

Him, then we learn the true joy, peace, and hope that comes through trusting Him. Then it becomes our deepest heart's desire to live according to His perfect plan for us.

There always will be questions. The key is to seek His answers, not our answers or answers from others.

We must come to a time in our relationship with our heavenly Father when we believe he can do all that He says He can do. We have lived in doubt from the moment of our loss.

There comes a point when we must believe that in spite of the pain, in spite of the doubt, in spite of the void that we have felt in our lives, we know, *beyond a shadow of a doubt*, that He has had and continues to have the desire for us to have a full and meaningful life once again with true purpose. But first, we must have the desire to know Him in a more personal and intimate way.

> Then I will give them a heart to know Me, that I am the LORD; and they shall be My people, and I will be their God, for they shall return to Me with their whole heart. (Jeremiah 24:7 NKJV)

He wants us to eagerly—almost with an urgent manner—seek His purpose for our lives every day, not just occasionally.

May I suggest a faith-walk journal? It's a place to write the most intimate details of this new journey with the Lord. A place where you can see your thoughts in black and white—the areas of doubt; the areas of walking in faith, not by sight, not by feelings, not by your purpose but His purpose and that you seek fervently that purpose through this journey of daily hope in Him.

Jot down those feelings—those times when you cannot see, those times when you cannot feel, those times when you see no purposes to it at all, yet you allow yourself to see how you can begin that walk in faith, believing that He is your Paraclete and will carry you through to the next step because of that faith.

Again, let's use the psalms to find those promises that He is there to carry you and be your protector.

> Because you are my help, I sing in the shadow of your wings. (Psalm 63:7 NIV)

How do you get to that place where you are no longer wandering without a clear direction and instead are singing for joy?

Simply by walking in faith.

Consider this acronym, FAITH: Freedom Abounds in Trusting Him

Do you want freedom from the bondage of grief? It's not easy and certainly won't be magical. It's a day-by-day walk, an intentional walk with true purpose as your goal. Give your faith-walk journal a name—a name significant to you. May I suggest a scriptural name? You start out each day with that same scripture and burn it in your heart! Mine would look something like this:

> The LORD will fulfill his purpose for me. (Psalm 138:8 ESV)

(By the way, this hangs above my bathroom mirror.) I start my day with a prayer entry and end my day with a prayer entry. Why? Because God wants us to talk to Him.

First Thoughts: Lord, what is Your purpose for me today?

Then I jot down those daily things that are set before me and how I should seek His purpose in them for my faith walk.

Last Thoughts: Lord, this is what I saw in my faith walk today.

Then I jot down those things that showed His purposes and how my faith walk made it possible to take that next step.

What about those days when you find no purpose? Once again, ask Him. Remember that He already knows your thoughts before you write them down, so if it is not a pretty day, share your heart. He can only show you whatever you are willing to open yourself up to His revelation. Remember: it is your choice.

I will provide the first ten days of your faith-walk journal. After that, go to any place that sells journals—many stores have them—and find one that looks like it would draw you to its pages each day.

I started a journal for each season of my journey, so I had many that were started and ended in the middle of the book. That's OK too; it's just more for you to hide. That is where a "Cathy" steps into your life. But allow it to be for you, that tool you need for your day to be successful, as you commune with God. That should be your ultimate purpose: to commune with God daily.

My Daily Faith Walk with the Lord

The LORD will fulfill his purpose for me. (Psalm 138:8 ESV)

Date:_____

First Thoughts: Lord, what is Your purpose for me today?

_____

_____

_____

_____

_____

Last Thoughts: Lord, this is what I saw in my faith walk today:

_____

_____

_____

_____

_____

God's Word for the Day:

In you, Lord my God, I put my trust. (Psalm 25:1 NIV)

My Daily Faith Walk with the Lord

The LORD will fulfill his purpose for me. (Psalm 138:8 ESV)

Date:_____

First Thoughts: Lord, what is Your purpose for me today?

_____

_____

_____

_____

_____

Last Thoughts: Lord, this is what I saw in my faith walk today:

_____

_____

_____

_____

_____

God's Word for the Day:

I will walk by faith, even when I cannot see. (2 Corinthians. 5:7 NIV)

My Daily Faith Walk with the Lord

The LORD will fulfill his purpose for me. (Psalm 138:8 ESV)

Date:_____

First Thoughts: Lord, what is Your purpose for me today?

_____

_____

_____

_____

_____

Last Thoughts: Lord, this is what I saw in my faith walk today:

_____

_____

_____

_____

_____

God's Word for the Day:

They that wait upon the Lord, shall renew their strength. (Isaiah 40:31 NIV)

My Daily Faith Walk with the Lord

The LORD will fulfill his purpose for me. (Psalm 138:8 ESV)

Date:_____

First Thoughts: Lord, what is Your purpose for me today?

_____

_____

_____

_____

_____

Last Thoughts: Lord, this is what I saw in my faith walk today:

_____

_____

_____

_____

_____

God's Word for the Day:

Trust in the Lord with all your heart. (Proverbs 3:5 NIV)

My Daily Faith Walk with the Lord

The LORD will fulfill his purpose for me. (Psalm 138:8 ESV)

Date:_____

First Thoughts: Lord, what is Your purpose for me today?

_____

_____

_____

_____

_____

Last Thoughts: Lord, this is what I saw in my faith walk today:

_____

_____

_____

_____

_____

God's Word for the Day:

Whatever you ask for in prayer, believe that you have received it, and it will be yours. (Mark 11:24 NIV)

My Daily Faith Walk with the Lord

The LORD will fulfill his purpose for me. (Psalm 138:8 ESV)

Date:_____

First Thoughts: Lord, what is Your purpose for me today?

_____

_____

_____

_____

_____

Last Thoughts: Lord, this is what I saw in my faith walk today:

_____

_____

_____

_____

_____

God's Word for the Day:

I am holding you by your right hand, I, The Lord your God and I say to you, Don't be afraid; I am with you. (Isaiah 41:13 NIV)

My Daily Faith Walk with the Lord

The LORD will fulfill his purpose for me. (Psalm 138:8 ESV)

Date:_____

First Thoughts: Lord, what is Your purpose for me today?

_____

_____

_____

_____

_____

Last Thoughts: Lord, this is what I saw in my faith walk today:

_____

_____

_____

_____

_____

God's Word for the Day:

What is faith? It is confidence in what we hope for and assurance about what we do not see. (Hebrews 11:1 NIV)

My Daily Faith Walk with the Lord

The LORD will fulfill his purpose for me. (Psalm 138:8 ESV)

Date:_____

First Thoughts: Lord, what is Your purpose for me today?

_____

_____

_____

_____

_____

Last Thoughts: Lord, this is what I saw in my faith walk today:

_____

_____

_____

_____

_____

God's Word for the Day:

For every promise from God shall surely come true. (Luke 1:37 NIV)

My Daily Faith Walk with the Lord

The Lord will fulfill his purpose for me. (Psalm 138:8 ESV)

DATE:_____

First Thoughts: Lord, what is Your purpose for me today?

_____

_____

_____

_____

_____

Last Thoughts: Lord, this is what I saw in my faith walk today:

_____

_____

_____

_____

_____

God's Word for the Day:

He heals the brokenhearted and binds up their wounds. (Psalm 147:3 NIV)

My Daily Faith Walk with the Lord

The LORD will fulfill his purpose for me. (Psalm 138:8 ESV)

Date:_____

First Thoughts: Lord, what is Your purpose for me today?

_____

_____

_____

_____

_____

Last Thoughts: Lord, this is what I saw in my faith walk today:

_____

_____

_____

_____

_____

God's Word for the Day:

My God turns my darkness into light. (Psalm 18:28 NIV)

Faith, Not Sight

We must find beauty in the walk,
not just the destination. Psalm 91:2 speaks clearly
to my heart: "This I declare about the Lord: He
alone is my refuge, my place of safety; He is my
God, and I trust him" (NLT).

And then again, in Psalm 91:4—"His faithful
promises are your armor" (NLT).

Amen and amen.

Find comfort in his Word. All that you need
to walk this journey is there—His story in black
and white.

He wants to walk this journey with us, hand
in hand, but he is not a demanding God. He is a
loving God with patience, love, and forgiveness,
as we struggle to understand the process of this
grief we are experiencing.

> Every morning tell him, "Thank
> you for your kindness," and
> every evening rejoice in all his
> faithfulness.
> —Psalm 92:2 (TLB)

Dedication

This book was written to all of you who have crossed my path, as I have journeyed to tell you my story, while carrying your own stories in your heart, I thank you. For taking that chance in opening yourselves up to see what God might have to say to you between these pages as you have become vulnerable to the deepest pain one can experience, I thank you. Because you have come to realize the true meaning of unconditional love and recognize that God's healing Grace is necessary to bring, JOY, HOPE and PEACE to your life again, I pray that this journey of walking a NEW KIND OF NORMAL, will be made easier as He carries you through.